THIS BOOK BELONGS TO

DOG

TRAINING

in 10 Minutes

D∙G

TRAINING

in 10 Minutes

Written and Illustrated by

CAROL LEA BENJAMIN

with photographs by Stephen J. Lennard
and the author

HOWELL BOOK HOUSE
NEW YORK

A Simon & Schuster Macmillan Company
1633 Broadway
New York, NY 10019-6785

Book design by George J. McKeon

Library of Congress Cataloging-in-Publication Data
Benjamin, Carol Lea.
    Dog training in ten minutes / written and illustrated by Carol Lea
Benjamin ; with photographs by Stephen J. Lennard and the author.
        p.   cm.
    ISBN 0-87605-471-8
    1. Dogs—Training.   I. Title.
SF431.B4215   1997
636.7'0887—dc20   96-23752
                                                                  CIP

Printed in the United States of America
10 9 8 7 6 5 4 3 2

Some of the drawings and part of the text of this book were previously published in a
slightly different form in the *AKC Gazette* in May 1987, February 1993, June 1993,
September 1993, October 1993, April 1994, June 1994 and April 1995.

For Laurie Nelson Lehey,
good friend

and for Dexter and Flash,
sit, stay, come, roll over, *good* dogs

CONTENTS

ACKNOWLEDGMENTS

Many thanks to:

Donald McCaig, Gene Sheninger, Larry Berg, Stephen Joubert, Arthur Haggerty and dear absent friend Job Michael Evans for invaluable dog talk at the highest level;

Sean Frawley, Dominique DeVito and Beth Adelman at Howell Book House;

Gail Hochman, who I took straight to the dogs;

Richard Siegel, Polly DeMille and Gina Spadafori for friendship beyond measure;

Stephen, my sweetie;

Odo, Annie, Magic, Holden, Katy, Yankee, Dexter and to Ollie. Still missing you, Red.

With hugs and kisses for Victoria and Zachary Elijah.

A NOTE ABOUT GENDER

Some writers, in an attempt to be politically correct, refer to a dog whose gender has not been mentioned previously as *it*. Because I am able to tell from a great distance whether a dog is male or female, and because I see vast differences in the behavior of males and females, I am unable to think of a dog, neutered or natural, as an *it*.

Other writers, to compensate for the fact that dogs were referred to as *he* for years, as if there were no bitches about, use an affirmative action approach, referring to all dogs as *she*.

In this book, using a personal approach, because having a dog is deeply personal, I have decided to refer to all dogs other than specifically named dogs as *he*, because at the time of this writing a *he* is what I've got.

Let no person take offense, as none is implied.

INTRODUCTION

This is a book for every busy person who has a dog. Even if you have little time for the *why* of dog behavior, you still need the *how*—how to get your dog to sit, stay, come when called, close a door, give a kiss and turn around in the tub so that you can wash his other side.

When work is long and time is short, you need a kind, quick, effective way to educate your dog for his safety, your sanity and for the closeness working together creates. Happily, you can teach your dog just about anything, working only ten minutes at a time.

Still, it is best to remember that training is not merely something to practice for ten minutes a day, nor are commands an end in themselves. Training is best when integrated into the life of owner and dog from the outset of the relationship. The point of

training is not so much what it teaches the dog to *do*, but what it helps the dog *become*—the most evolved, interesting, communicative, playful friend he can be given his genetic makeup and inherited character.

Because most new skills will take time to gel—not so much like the way a pudding sets in the refrigerator, but by use—one tip for saving time is not to teach your dog anything neither of you needs.

On the other hand, the more you teach your dog, the faster and more easily he can learn. So figuring out why you *need* your dog to wave good-bye, jump over your legs or back up on command may be worth your while.

The one thing you cannot accomplish in ten minutes that you thought would take an hour is exercising your dog. Sadly, if there's no time in your life to exercise your dog and no one else to do it for you for either love or money, it is probably not the right time for you to have a dog. Cheating a dog of the chance to use his mind and body with delightful abandon, preferably out-of-doors, is buying trouble on the installment plan. Eventually you and your dog will pay the price.

Even here, we offer help. Special ten-minute workouts that address your dog's need for

mental and physical exercise are included in this book and can easily be integrated into your daily routine. These will count as part of your dog's daily exercise.

In addition, once you have taught your dog not to pull, some of his need to exercise, socialize and explore can coincide with your own necessary outings.

As for the rest, the time you spend with a *trained* dog, tossing a ball, watching him romp with his fellows or taking him for a run and a swim at the beach after hours, he'll be such a pleasure to be with that you will want to spend the time with him. An obedient, well-exercised dog, you will see, is a more excellent companion than you might now imagine.

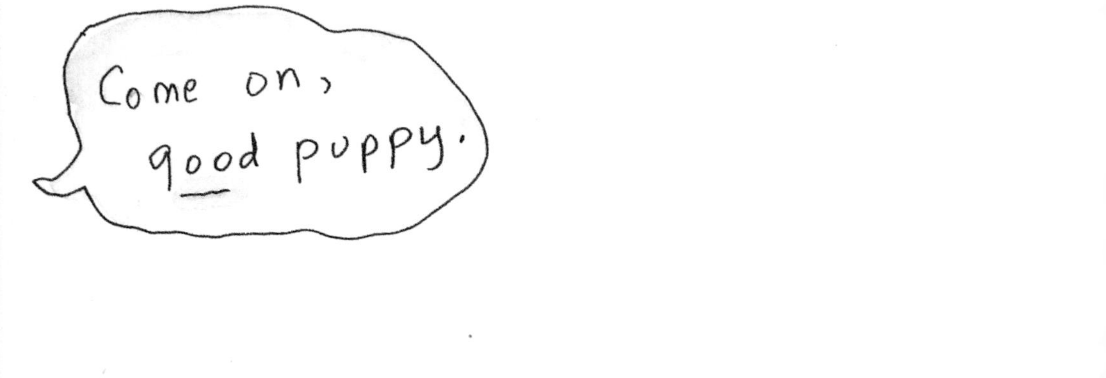
Come on, good puppy.

PART ONE

Preparation

 # One

Sad, Mad, Bad, Glad: How to Know What Your Dog Is Feeling

If your dog were a cartoon, you'd always know what he was feeling.

 His eyebrows would point up to show worry.

Droplets of sweat would fly out to the side when he was anxious.

He'd look positively wicked when he had naughty thoughts or, worse yet, had done a naughty deed.

He'd have a canine version of that have-a-nice-day grin when he was happy…

…and a little balloon would appear occasionally over his head to reveal significant inner dialogue.

3

If you want to know what a *real* dog is feeling, almost what he's thinking, his body language will tell you. It can be as clear a message as those delivered by cartoon dogs.

A tucked tail, a play bow, a submissive show of chest and belly, legs apart in an aggressive stance—these tell a reliable story. Body language reveals the individual, each gesture a tale of irrevocable truth.

BODY LANGUAGE, ILLUSTRATED AND EXPLAINED

Fear

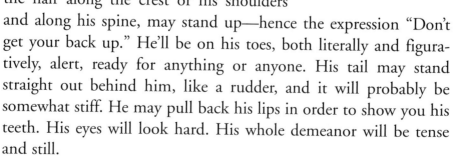

In order to protect himself from real or imagined dangers, the fearful dog holds everything tight to his body. His ears may be down or back, close to his head. His tail may be tucked. He may crouch, rounding his back and holding his head low. He may tremble.

Aggression

The aggressive dog tries to gain advantage by making himself appear as large as possible. His ears may be up and slightly forward. His hackles, the hair along the crest of his shoulders and along his spine, may stand up—hence the expression "Don't get your back up." He'll be on his toes, both literally and figuratively, alert, ready for anything or anyone. His tail may stand straight out behind him, like a rudder, and it will probably be somewhat stiff. He may pull back his lips in order to show you his teeth. His eyes will look hard. His whole demeanor will be tense and still.

Dominance

The dominant dog will show his dominance toward you by staring, mounting (even when it's spring, if your dog mounts your leg, trust me, it isn't love), disobedience, shoving, always trying to get ahead of you, usurping your favorite spot, ignoring you, demanding attention. The dominant dog may display dominance toward other dogs by teeing up. That is, he will rest his chin or his paws on the other dog's shoulders, which delivers the clear message that he is top dog. He may also try to mount the other dog. He may raise his hackles, show his teeth, growl or even attack.

Submission

The submissive dog uses ritualistic postures that all dogs, domesticated and wild, and even wolves, understand. The postures say, "Hey, I'm no threat; don't attack me." The submissive dog may crouch, paw the air, grin (wrinkle the muzzle and show the teeth in a sort of embarrassed smile), roll over and even urinate. Most puppies will act submissive around older dogs, especially those they do not know. Some females retain submissive behavior patterns throughout their lives.

Friendliness

The friendly dog will look relaxed and loose, wagging his tail, wiggling his body, panting or offering his paw. He may play bow, to you or to another dog, dropping his chest to the ground

and leaving his rump and wagging tail in the air. He may pounce in order to begin a game. His eyes look friendly, relaxed, calm and round. They arc not pinched with fear nor hard and still. His hackles are down. His ears may be slightly back or up and alert. He exudes all those qualities that draw us to his species.

Because your dog is without a complex verbal language, he is already an expert at nonverbal messages. He will let you know what he is feeling by using the postures illustrated above. Not surprisingly, he will also know what you are feeling. Using *his* understanding of body language as well as his uncanny ability to feel the emotions of those around him, he will know when *you* are sad, mad or glad. That makes it important, when working with your dog, to keep your actions and feelings in concert and appropriate to the task at hand. Do not correct your dog and smile at the same time, as some people (those somewhat uncomfortable with being in charge) tend to do. If you are not in charge of your dog, who will be? By the same token, don't tell your dog he's perfect when your face is registering anger from another cause. If you are very upset, don't work with your dog until you feel better. He'll know what you are feeling and be confused by your mixed messages.

Reading a dog's feelings and helping him to understand you by sending your own messages simply and clearly to him will save you lots of training time. You won't mistake momentary fear for a stubborn unwillingness to obey. And when your praise comes with not only a pat but a smile as well, your dog will knock himself out to earn it again and again. With improved communication, training will proceed as quickly as your dog's age, intelligence and character will allow.

Two

Dressing Your Dog for Work

When I began working as a professional trainer, it was easy to dress a dog for work. You got a collar and a leash and you did the job.

Now there are head halters, no-pull harnesses, extendible leads and shock collars. So many choices cause concern. After all, the wrong equipment may be ineffective or, worse, inhumane.

Lots of these devices come with the guarantee that they will make the job easier, practically no work at all. When something sounds too good to be true, it usually is. *Caveat emptor.* Experience has shown me that as heavier or more complicated equipment is used—the prong collar and head halter, for example—the tendency is to rely on the gear for help rather than to work on the relationship. Yet what I've seen in my training work is that the relationship is precisely what needs fixing. This is accomplished best and most quickly through improving the communication between master and dog, not by adding more paraphernalia.

7

When professional trainers or pet owners rely on more equipment and more complicated equipment, they simply do not get the job done. Instead of winning the dog's attention and respect, instead of improving the quality of communication, equipment—much of which is meant to be used temporarily—is used permanently. In other words, the owner is relying on stuff rather than finding ways to engage the dog's mind.

My own belief is that the dog should understand everything that is happening to him, just as he did when his mother taught him the basic lessons of puppyhood. Therefore, in order to correct my dog, I never throw anything at him but my voice. I never zap a dog with electricity or stun him with noise. I don't use devices to get a dog's attention or keep him off my furniture.

Like any dog's first teacher, his mother, my most important training aids are confidence, affection, a willingness to set limits and the habit of concentrating fully on the task at hand. Because the dog himself is old-fashioned, understanding his world and behaving much in the way that dogs always have, I am content with old-fashioned equipment—basically, a collar and leash. By choosing a minimum of equipment, I keep the dog's focus, and my own, on our relationship.

In addition, the proper equipment should increase the possibility of good communication, should never leave the dog confused as to the source of praise and correction, should augment understanding between owner and dog and should help decrease, never increase, stress in the dog.

So when yet another new device comes on the market, I ask myself, how much *stuff* should I need in order to get my dog to pay attention to me and obey a few simple commands?

This said, here is all you need to train your dog:

A basic *buckle collar,* with ID, should be worn by your dog when he is loose in the house and you are home, as well as anytime he is outside. A dog without a collar is difficult to correct, should a correction be necessary. But even for the near perfect dog, the feel and weight of a collar are a reminder of a dog's secure, loved position as an appropriately subordinate pack member.

A *nylon slip collar* is ideal for training all dogs, big and small, with the exception of toy breeds and any dog with a diagnosed medical condition that precludes even the slightest pressure on his neck. The nylon collar, slipped high on the neck, allows for the smallest of corrections to be highly effective.

A *four- or six-foot leather leash* is handsome, durable and easy on the hands. For all but advanced training situations, it is preferable to have the dog close rather than far away.

Three

Teaching Friendly Respect

T he perfect way to begin an appropriate relationship with a dog is to play a following game. When your dog follows you—around the house, around your yard or, on leash, around your neighborhood—you are, figuratively and literally, the leader and he, the follower. This simple, easy-to-practice exercise sets the tone for your life together.

Once your dog learns to respect you by following you and thus regarding you as his leader (alpha), he'll pay attention and you will be able to teach him what you need to rapidly. Without attention, you cannot teach. Without respect, there is no attention.

Will your gentle leadership and training make your dog lose his charm, his naturalness, his spirit? Humane training has never broken the spirit of any dog—bad habits, yes, but not his spirit.

11

So no matter how old your dog is, or how long you've had him, let's begin at the beginning, with a game of alpha in motion.

"FOLLOW ME"

Always begin at home. Use your voice, a favorite ball or a squeak toy as lures and simply, and I do mean this, walk through your house, calling your dog to follow you. Be as playful and energetic as you like, always attracting the dog to follow along, never carping, scaring, shouting. Training should be fun for both of you. So don't forget to praise as you go.

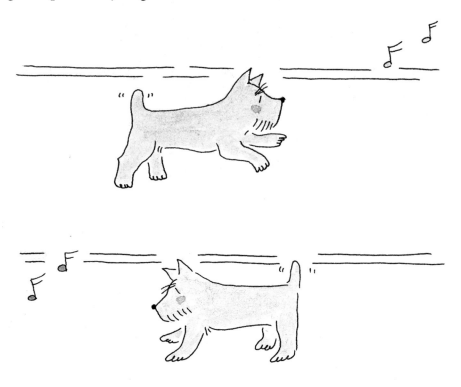

After a week indoors, five or ten minutes in the morning and another five or ten in the evening, move out-of-doors. If you have a fenced yard, you won't need a leash. If you have no fence or no yard, leash your dog and continue to *play* the follow-me game.

It may not look like much because it's so easy. But later on, follow me almost miraculously tightens up to become "Heel," which used to be one of the most difficult and time-consuming commands to teach. So stick with it.

If your dog is a brand-new puppy, still getting used to his leash, follow *him*, then lure him with your voice or a toy to follow *you*, back and forth, back and forth, off leash indoors, on leash out-of-doors.

For grown or half-grown dogs, and for puppies as they grow, once the dog follows well and willingly, with his tail wagging, begin to change your direction as you go. Tap your leg, squeak his toy, call his name, whistle, inspiring him to change his direction and follow you. One way. The other way. One way. The other way. Praise your dog for all signs of cooperation and attentiveness.

After a week of short sessions, five or ten minutes at a time at most, make another change. Now when you change your mind and turn to walk in the opposite direction, don't lure your dog to turn and come along. Don't tap your leg, call his name, squeak a toy or whistle. Just go.

Suddenly, you are no longer predictable to your dog. He has to watch you carefully. If not, he's going to give himself a correction. You have cleverly transferred the *responsibility* for paying attention to your dog. In fact, this is precisely what we are after.

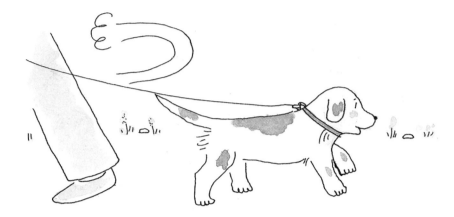

It is a dog's job to pay careful attention to his master. This means, eventually, he will turn with you rather than charging on ahead or lagging behind. He will stop and wait when you stop to chat with a neighbor, look in a store window, wait for the light to change or buy a newspaper. He won't trip you on the stairs—or get stepped on— because he'll watch your feet. And most important, as the object of his attention, you, not he, now have the role of alpha, or top dog, the very role you must have in order to educate your dog.

"Follow me" is the basis of two essentials: that the human, not the dog, must be the leader, and that the dog must learn to walk properly when out on the leash, taking on the responsibility of paying attention to his master's intent. Being in charge is vital, no matter what size dog you have. But if your dog is small, the following game may be all you need to teach him to walk well on leash. And if he's not small, not to worry, there's lots more to come.

Four

Teaching via Praise and Correction

R esponding to your dog's behavior with appropriate praise and correction teaches him two indispensable lessons: how to win your approval and, just as important, how to avoid your disapproval. As his caretaker, it is not only your right but your obligation to positively reinforce behaviors that are safe or even laudable and negatively reinforce those that are annoying or even dangerous.

You may wonder, because knowing how we feel is one of the things dogs do best, why do we need to remind them of what they already know? Surely every dog knows when his owner is pleased and when he is annoyed or even angry. Reminding your dog anyway does several things. It reinforces his con-cept of what is appropri-ate behavior and what isn't. It is also how we teach our dogs skills and vocabulary. Of course, without reinforcement your dog will still learn. But he may not learn the things you want him to.

Even learned behaviors may fade or become sloppy without the reinforcement of occasional praise and correction. If you teach your dog to come promptly when you call him, and when he does you never praise him for doing so, he may stop obeying you. He may slow down his response. He may wait for a second, third or fourth command. He may act as if he were deaf and not respond at all. If you teach him not to pick up food in the street, then never remind him of this taboo, a powerful enticement might just inspire him to forget he's not supposed to give in to temptation.

Suppose your dog is doing just what he feels like doing—playing nicely with a buddy, being gentle with a child, exploring someplace new in an appropriate, civilized manner—and what he is doing already gives him pleasure. Who needs you to mouth "Good dog"? He does.

Suppose he is doing the very work he is genetically driven to do, a task that gives him utter satisfaction—pointing birds, herding sheep, pulling a cart, dispatching a rodent. Who needs you to tell him "Good boy"? He does.

Praise and correction, with a greater emphasis on praise, are an important part of the conversation between a person and a dog, part of the cement of the relationship, part of the recognition that *even when the work is its own reward,* appropriate reinforcement is what makes two individuals become a working partnership. It is precisely by monitoring your dog's behavior, by commenting on it, as it were, that you keep yourself in your dog's consciousness, and by doing so you nurture not only good behavior on his part but the relationship itself.

No matter if it's work or play, whether your dog is just having fun, God bless him, or if what he's doing is as genetically driven as is herding sheep for the Border Collie, if you quietly insert yourself into the activity, something that otherwise would have little or nothing to do with you, you end up strengthening your ability to work with your dog.

Do not be a pest. Don't badger or talk constantly. Merely introduce yourself into your dog's activities in a gentle, spare way so that your relationship with him becomes part of what he does, even when what he does is genetically driven and gives him satisfaction. Think

about it this way: If you are not included in what your dog likes to do, all that's left for you is to be included in the things he doesn't like so well, the things that are difficult for him, annoying or painful. In that case, he might like you involved in what he does about as much as the dog who gets to ride in the family car only when he needs to go to the veterinarian likes to ride in the car.

In order to live and work well with you, your dog must learn that pleasing you is Job One. Coming from a person who feels her citizenship will be revoked if every day of her dog's life is not a marvelous adventure, this does not seem unreasonable. After all, the fact that what your dog is doing pleases *you* does not in any way mean it's not also pleasing the hell out of *him*.

PRAISE AND CORRECTION AS TEACHING TOOLS

Neither praise nor correction should take anywhere near ten minutes of your time, even on those occasions when your dog is superbly good or bordering on disreputable. Nor will you need any special equipment or food treats in order to reinforce your dog's responses and behaviors. Your voice, because it is an expression of what you feel, is powerful enough to train any dog. Because most dogs have excellent hearing, you can speak softly to your dog, using your normal tone for praise and a deeper, growly—but not loud—tone for correction. Remember, it's your dog's job to pay attention to you, so you need not shout.

You may be wondering, why not use food as a reward in addition to pats and "Good dog"? When you educate in such a way that your dog's focus is on pleasing you, you become his beacon in a dark place, the brightest light in a place filled with sunlight. This bond is real. It is not based on disposable rewards. After all, anyone can offer your dog a treat. Only you can offer him the affection of his alpha.

Why should your dog care about your approval or disapproval, or care what you feel? Not because he loves you. Because you are alpha. In fact, when you become alpha, your dog's gentle leader, he'll *adore* you. At that point, what you feel becomes paramount to your dog.

THE TWO SIDES OF ALPHA

Respect

Adoration

An expression of your pleasure positively reinforces desired behavior, letting your dog know precisely what you want him to do. So when your dog is obedient, good or brave, reward him with a warm "Good dog!", a delicious pat, a quick hug or all three.

An expression of your displeasure negatively reinforces undesired behavior, letting your dog know precisely what you don't want him to do. So when your dog is disobedient, cheeky or naughty, tell him "*Bad* dog!"

If your dog is disobedient when you are working him on leash, simply pop the leash, release it immediately and simultaneously tell him "*No!*" Now quickly show him again what he must do to gain your praise and continue working with him in a cheerful manner, being sure to end your 10-minute session on a high note, that is, with a command he knows and does well and that can legitimately win him some warm pats and praise.

Suppose your dog is horrible. Suppose, for example, he growls at you. Don't hit him, throw anything at him, scare him or hurt him. The very last thing you want to do is inspire your dog to defend himself. You want to educate him. So, *if you are not afraid of your dog,* grasp his collar and cheeks in your hands, holding tight, and bring his face in the direction of yours, but not close enough for his teeth to reach you should that heinous idea occur to him. Now, chew him out. Seriously. This correction should take no more than ten seconds. But in those ten seconds, your justifiable anger is pointing right at your dog, and because you are holding his rotten face, he can't turn away from it.

I have never met a dog for whom this correction was considered less than physical correction. Amazingly, for a pet dog, the genuine full-steam disapproval of a beloved owner is the worst punishment imaginable. After reading your dog the riot act, crate him (see chapter 5 for crate training) or isolate him in another room for half an hour to give both of you time to calm down. When you are ready to deal with him again, do so with caution.

If your dog is aggressive toward you or other people, you may want to hire a professional trainer or, at the very least, take him to a group obedience class. However, if he growls for the first time and you correct him and his response is superb, as in, Oh God, I didn't know I shouldn't do *that*, you may very well be able to continue working with him yourself. Many dogs corrected properly for a first try at aggression give it up. Some do not, and with those, as well as with a dog you are already afraid of, professional help *is* advised.

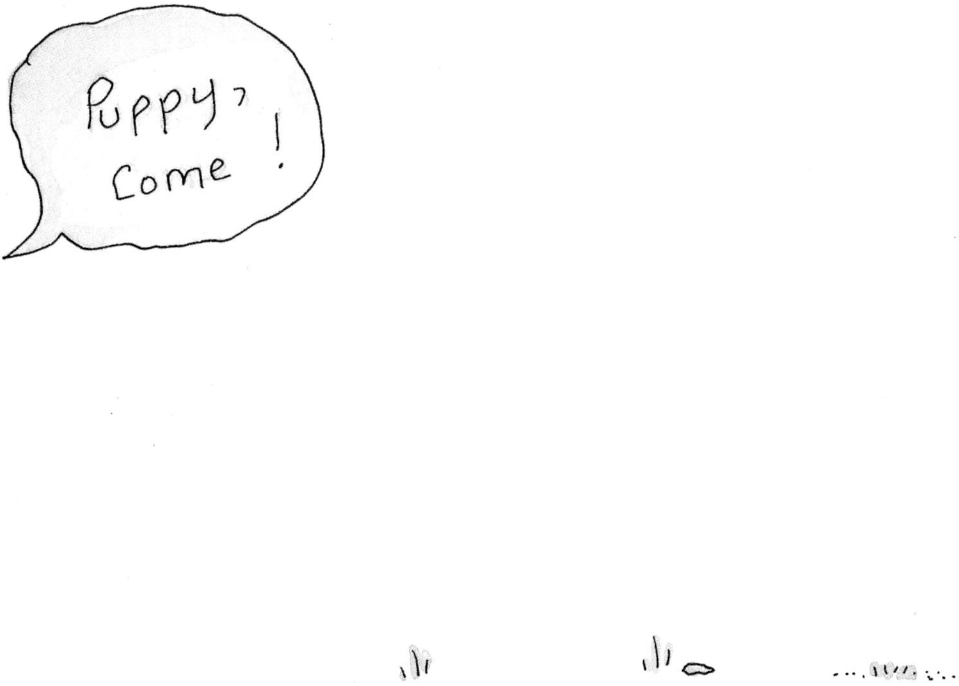
Puppy, come!

Part Two
Education

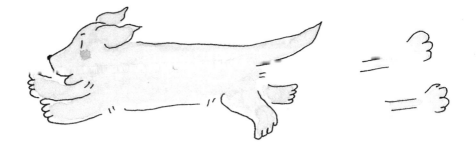

Five

The Bare Minimum

Suppose you've decided you don't want to train your dog. You love him exactly the way he is.

If you've gotten this far, you already know that every dog needs to learn *some* lessons in order to be part of a human family. Hopefully, you have already taught him to follow you so he pays attention and is beginning to think of you as his leader.

Even if you have no interest in heeling, down/stay or games, you probably *do* want one more thing. Unfortunately, the one thing most people who don't want to train their dogs want is for their dogs to come, off leash. This is usually no more possible than building a house without a foundation. In order to have a dog come when called when he's out of doors in an unfenced area, you will, like a builder, need to have a foundation. You need a dog trained reliably on leash before you begin.

What, then, would be an attainable bare minimum for a good pet? I would consider a dog who had the minimum vocabulary of *no* and *okay,* didn't bite, was house-trained, didn't pull and would sit and give his paw, a dog that one could live with nicely. You may agree. Or, like me, you may want more. No matter. Even if you don't yet know how far you want to go with your dog, this is the right place to begin.

"No" and "Okay"

"No" and "Okay" are tools of the trade. "No" is a growl. It warns and stops. "Okay" is a love song. It gives permission. Delivered with the proper tone of voice, a deep tone for "No," a normal or slightly higher pitch for "Okay," these two little words will be as useful to you in educating your dog as a collar and leash.

GROWING UP UNAGGRESSIVE

I have often worked for owners with biting dogs, and I guess I will never get over the shock of hearing one say, "Except for the biting, he's a perfectly good dog." With all my heart, I feel a biting dog is a perfectly *bad* dog.

If you are about to choose a dog, and having a gentle, friendly dog is important to you, choose a breed that is known to be affable with both humans and dogs, and select a puppy from the middle of the litter, neither a shy one nor the most dominant pup. Whether you see a litter or a single pup, choose a puppy that is friendly but respectful, one that comes to you but not one that marches all over you.

When you raise your puppy, be sure to social-ize him well. A good program of socialization means lots and lots of experience, most of it positive and out in the world, away from home. Your puppy will not only become comfortable with other

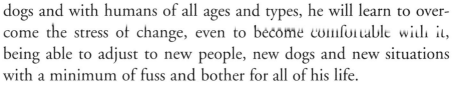

dogs and with humans of all ages and types, he will learn to over-come the stress of change, even to become comfortable with it, being able to adjust to new people, new dogs and new situations with a minimum of fuss and bother for all of his life.

What if your dog is aggressive toward you or other people? If your adult dog already has a history of aggression toward you, he must be retrained and corrected for any aggressive displays. If this is the case at your home, I would be less than responsible to tell you to work without professional help. But if your dog has just made his first try at aggression or if you are raising a dog and want to pre-vent aggression, the following advice will help.

You must become alpha. Do the follow-me game, and some very basic training, to teach your dog the appropriate hierarchy, that which he is naturally able to understand. You, not he, are on top of the pyramid. This means that when you take him places, your presence will make him feel relaxed rather than edgy. Underneath the basic commands a trust is built, a confidence that you as your dog's leader will never take him into harm's way. Trust is a great tension reliever.

Tension should be your guide in judging whether or not your dog will be prone to aggression in any given situation. It is the most accurate precursor to an aggressive display. If you know your dog well, you'll easily be able to both see and feel when his level of tension rises because of the presence of another male, because you are handling or brushing him in a way that bothers him, because there is a bitch in season nearby, because a new situation or setting makes him uncomfortable. Tension manifests itself in a stiffening of the body, and a kind of stillness, including a lack of motility in the eyes.

The more quickly you can recognize this, the faster you can do something to offset it.

To prevent possible aggression, if your dog gets tense from handling, nail cutting, grooming or even a bath, you'll need to desensitize him to these activities. You might, for example, cut one or two nails at a time. No law says you have to do all his nails the same day. Build his ability to be handled by working for brief periods and using lots of warm praise for his "bravery."

Suppose your dog's level of tension builds in obedience class, from corrections, from control or from the presence of other dogs. Work him for five or ten minutes and then take him away from the group, out-of-doors if the class is an indoor one. Move him quickly, do some playful, cheerful heeling and recalls. Then take him back to class and work another ten or twelve minutes. When he gets tense, do not go for control. Instead, remove him and exercise him. The movement and the separation from the other dogs will alleviate his tension. As you work this way, you will increase his ability to handle situations that now make him uptight.

Be warned: Even if you do everything right, some dogs will not tolerate other dogs. Some males, when they reach adolescence, become aggressive toward other males. Some bitches may become intolerant of other females. Less frequently, bitches will attack dogs and vice versa. Once my dog Dexter was flattened by a huge female who disliked displays of male passion. He looked like one of those cartoon characters that had been run over by a steamroller, his back on the ground, his neck exposed, his eyes averted. For one terrible moment, he looked like a piece of paper, a drawing of surrender. But the owner of the bitch was swift and Dexter was not injured. We were a safe distance away before I had enough saliva in my mouth to say thank you. With so many nice, friendly dogs around, why take chances with dogs who appear to have attitude problems?

If you want to be able to relax when out with your dog, why not · choose a breed that's easy with other dogs? Though of course there are exceptions, sporting dogs and hounds tend to be affable around other dogs. Terriers tend to be scrappy. Herding and working dogs range from friendly to indifferent to intolerant.

If you already have your dog, be realistic. If he's aggressive toward other dogs, be careful with him. Keep him on leash in the park, or walk him elsewhere, where fewer dogs gather. He can still be a great pet, as long as he's not aggressive to you.

Among males there is no way to make everyone buddies. Even if your male is affable with others, he may not like *everyone* and everyone will not accept him with equanimity. My dog loves to play with other males. He'll often choose the males over bitches. He longs to be one of the guys, to hang out, drink a beer, watch the game and talk to the TV set. Yet, when I take him to the dog run I watch carefully so that, should things get strained, I can remove him prior to the onset of any hostility. Aggressive behavior *toward* him could not only cause him injury, it could teach him to relate aggressively.

The more positive experiences your male has with other dogs, the less likely he is to view his fellows combatively. When leashed dogs meet, tight leashes create tension. To minimize tension, leashes should be held loosely. Should a pleasant one-on-one encounter turn tense, the more aggressive dog should always be removed first. Removing the less or nonaggressive dog first makes the more aggressive dog even bolder as he sees his foe retreat. Unfortunately, the person with the aggressive dog won't always have the sense to remove his dog first. In these cases, simply take your dog out of harm's way as quickly as possible. I have literally *flown* my seventy-one-pound tank out of the way of a growling dog. In this case, as with removing a Band-Aid, faster is better.

What happens if you breed your dog? A bitch may be more aggressive during her heat and after the birth of the litter. But, more than likely, she'll be her old self again after the puppies have been placed with other families. The male dog, however, once bred, is likely to become the quintessential cocky male. Even one stunning brush with biology can make him aggressive toward other males. He may become touchy, tense and hypersensitive to irritation from other males only when in the presence of a bitch in season, or permanently combative with other males and in need of careful monitoring. Some mellow few stay just as friendly as when they were innocent, happy to mate when the opportunity arises and to play with males and females alike between assignments. But if your dog is a pet, you are far better off leaving the breeding to the professionals.

Here are some guidelines for preventing and dealing with aggression:

- If your male is aggressive toward people or dogs, the best thing you can do is neuter him. It's not a panacea. Your dog will still need training. But neutering removes a lot of the tension from a dog's life, and tension, as we have seen, is closely connected to aggression.

- If your intact male doesn't attack but *gets* attacked, it's his male hormones inspiring the rivalry from other males. In this case, you may also want to consider neutering your dog.

- Avoid inflammatory situations, rivalry over a bitch or a bone, too many dogs in a small space, jealousy over or protection of the owner.

- Do not encourage your dog to harbor an overblown view of his own prowess. Do not let him socialize on a tight leash. Do not allow him to fence-fight with the dog next door. Never pet him to "calm him down" when he is aggressive. He will read the petting as praise. Correct him instead with a stern "No" and a pop on the leash.

- Monitor aggression. Limit the time your dog barks at the door. Correct any inappropriate display of aggression.

- Be realistic. If you already have an adult dog who is intolerant of or aggressive toward other dogs, you will probably not be able to change this. Do not, therefore, take your dog off leash where he can harm other dogs.

- Don't ignore aggression. Among dogs, a growl can be communication, a message from a higher-ranked dog that the lower-ranked dog, perhaps a puppy, is being a pest. But growling that leads to fighting requires action—neutering, avoiding other same-sex dogs, avoiding dominant dogs, whatever is causing the problem. Growling at humans is absolutely out of the question. Pet dogs should not think they can bully their owners in order to get their way. A dog who growls at you, at your friends or at benign strangers needs training, preferably with professional advice or help.

Note: Correcting *inappropriate* aggression will not dissuade your dog from protecting you if he is a protective dog to begin with, should a genuine need arise.

- Your dog knows how you feel, remember? So if your expectation is that he will be aggressive toward people or dogs, he might be. He might pick up your tension and become tense. If, on the other hand, you expect the best, give your dog leadership, training, lots of chances to play with other gentle dogs and socialize with friendly humans, and you have chosen a dog with good friendship potential, he need not grow up aggressive.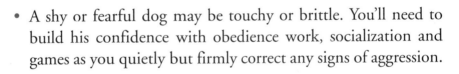

- A shy or fearful dog may be touchy or brittle. You'll need to build his confidence with obedience work, socialization and games as you quietly but firmly correct any signs of aggression.

- A confident dog is elastic. He does not fall apart when you have to tell him "No," nor will training and some rules dampen his spirit. He needs and can easily handle a firmer attitude. This does not imply that you should *hit* a confident, dominant or aggressive dog. Hitting tends to make dogs more aggressive, not less so.

- Do not play tug of war with your dog. It teaches a dog to grip hard, to pull things away from you, to bite and tug at objects he wants.

- Because, with dogs, you get out what you put in, do not rough house with your dog. Play active games—Frisbee, ball, jumping games—but not rough ones.

"SIT"

Teaching "Sit" is another way to get your dog to pay attention and understand that you are boss. "Sit" is also helpful when you need to get a collar on your dog, snap on a leash, cut toenails, clean ears, keep your dog still while you prepare his food, slow your dog down or get him to give you his paw.

Teach "Sit" as follows:

1. Say "Sit" as you attract your dog or puppy to look up at a toy or jingling keys. Many puppies and some dogs will automatically sit if they try to look over their heads. If your dog does, praise warmly.

2. Say "Sit" and with one hand gently lift your dog's chin as with the other hand you stroke his back, neck to tail and tuck your hand in beneath his rump, mechanically encouraging him to sit. Praise when he does.

3. Say "Sit" and pull up on your dog's leash (or collar) as you push gently down on his rump. This is a commonly used method that often works; however, most dogs push back when pushed. So this method is best used as a reminder after your dog has gotten the idea from one of the gentle methods above. When used as a reminder, a light touch on the rump will remind your dog to sit.

4. Once your dog begins to get the hang of "Sit," ask him to sit when he is highly motivated to obey you—before you place his dinner bowl on the floor, before you snap on his leash to take him out, before he hops into the car, before you toss a ball for him to chase. By using the "Sit," by *integrating* this command into your life with your dog, you will be teaching your dog to respond to the "Sit" command without spending much time at all on the teaching. Don't forget to reinforce your dog's cooperation with praise.

"Good dog!"

"GIVE YOUR PAW"

"Give your paw" is included as a bare essential for two reasons. First, when clients call me about training I always ask them what their dogs already do for them. Nearly all say, "He sits and gives his paw." I have gleaned from this that most dog owners find "Give your paw" to be an essential skill for a pet dog.

But "Give your paw" has a serious message beneath the trick. Pawing, the very gesture that humans think of as a trick, is a submissive gesture. All but the most dominant dogs do it on their own. It is a way of soliciting attention from a creature higher in the pecking order.

Therefore, teaching "Give your paw" and delighting everyone with this adorable trick reinforces your dog's position as a loved, cared for, submissive pack member, a cooperative group member, not an aggressor. By encouraging your dog to give his paw to a child, you are encouraging a safe and proper attitude toward children as well. This is why "Give your paw" really should be in every dog's repertoire.

1. Crouch in front of your dog and paw the air. He might imitate you. Gently take his paw and praise him.

2. Ask your dog to sit, crouch in front of him and scratch behind his ankle, between his large foot pad and his heel pad. This may make him loosen the foot or even lift it. Praise for any slight movement, grasping the foot and giving it a little shake.

3. With your dog on a sit, ask for his paw, holding your hand ready at his chest level to catch it, and tug sideways on his collar until he lifts the paw on the opposite side. Shake the paw and praise well.

"Right Now"
(The Laws of Nature as They Apply to House Training)

Although there are pet owners who couldn't care less about getting a dog to respond to commands, few are casual about house training. After all, living with a dog who urinates or defecates in your home is no fun. It's disgusting. Often, if the dog is an adult, it is the dog's charming way of letting you know in no uncertain terms that he, not you, is the one in charge. He's top dog, alpha, president and king, and the message—God help you—might even appear, like those mints at hotels, right on your pillow, thank you very much.

I always teach a dog to sit on command before I begin to house-train him. It is an easy way to teach a dog how to learn, concentrate and respect his owner's wishes. If your dog understands these essentials, his house training will proceed more efficiently.

If your dog is a puppy, you have a mechanical problem. He simply is not able to go for more than a few hours without relieving himself. You may think that because a puppy can go overnight and stay clean that he can also do this during the day. But during the day he is more active. And when a creature is up and about, digestion tends to be more active, too. Thus your little puppy will need access to the great outdoors more frequently than your half-grown or grown dog. Easy-to-use schedules and rules follow.

HOUSE TRAINING: THE LAWS OF NATURE

1. **What goes in must come out.** Puppies always need to relieve themselves after eating or drinking. Grown dogs need a chance to relieve themselves at least three times a day.

2. **It ain't over till it's over.** If you don't give your dog enough time to do everything he's got to do when he's out-of-doors, he may be forced to finish up indoors. If your dog goes out in your yard to relieve himself and you don't go along to see what he does and to praise him, you'll miss the chance to speed up his training with positive reinforcement and, worse, you won't have any idea if he went at all before you bring him back in.

3. **The only guaranteed way to house-train a dog is with a crate (den) and a humane schedule.** A dog is a den animal. Given half a chance, he will keep his den clean. A dog crate becomes your dog's den and teaches him to wait and stay clean between walks *if* he is on a humane schedule.

If your dog is not crate trained but you want to use a crate for house training or to prevent him from damaging your things or harming himself when you are unable to watch him, select a crate large enough for him to lie down comfortably in. If he's growing, take that into consideration but don't buy Grand Central Station to use as a crate.

Once you have the crate, take a few days to let your dog get used to it. Feed him in the crate. Let him sleep in the crate when he's really tired. Toss a biscuit in the crate and let him run in, take it and run out with it. Give him a special toy in the crate and close the door for a minute at a time, then two, then five.

Do not put your dog in the crate and leave the house until he's used to it and regards it as his den. And never leave him crated all day long. For safety's sake, remove his collar when he is going into his crate and put it on again when you let him out.

PUPPY SCHEDULE

- Wake up, jump into clothes, walk puppy.

- Shower, dress, have breakfast, feed puppy and walk him again.

- Play follow me, let puppy chase a ball, crate puppy.

  – Puppy stays in crate three to four hours at most.

  – Walk puppy, train puppy, play with puppy, crate puppy.

- Repeat steps above all day long, inserting your puppy's other meals into the schedule just prior to a walk. For very young puppies, see first part of the schedule for feed/walk.

- Crate overnight.

ADULT DOG SCHEDULE

- Wake up, get dressed, walk dog.

- Keep dog out of crate for up to one hour, then crate dog for up to four or five hours. Repeat throughout the day, making sure that the adult dog gets training and exercise when he is out of the crate. The adult dog can eat before his late-afternoon walk.

- Crate overnight.

HOUSE TRAINING: THE RULES

1. Name it. ("Right now!" works.)
2. Praise it. ("Yuck" isn't praise.)
3. Scoop it.
4. Dump it.
5. Stick to your dog's schedule.
6. Be patient.
7. Be attentive.
8. Remember, even *you* had to get "house trained" once upon a time.

TIMESAVING TIP

If you put a towel or mat in the crate of an unhousebroken dog, the dog may urinate on the cloth, push it to a corner and lie down in the clean part of the crate. To avoid this, and speed training, put nothing in the crate with the puppy other than a chew toy.

Now is the time to remember that this book promises that you will be able to train your dog working ten minutes at a time. However, if you have a puppy, there will be many ten-minute sessions a day. Puppies require a lot of monitoring, educating and stimulation. In addition, the dog who has been allowed to grow to adulthood unhousebroken will need time and attention from someone in order to get reeducated. You cannot crate an adult dog all day long and think you are doing right by your pet. However, your pet can be walked and exercised by someone else, like your kid, your neighbor or a dog walker until he is retrained.

HOW TO STOP YOUR DOG FROM PULLING

There are two ways to stop a dog from pulling. Both work. However, one is incredibly easier than the other.

1. When your dog pulls on his leash, you can pull back. Just like most humans, when you pull a dog, he'll put everything he's got into pulling the other way. If your dog weighs more than fifteen or twenty pounds, this is hard work. You won't like it. Not only that, when I do it, it makes me feel mean. Occasionally, well-meaning, nosy people even tell me I *am* mean for pulling my dog.

2. When your dog pulls on his leash, you can accomplish what you want by using the dog's force instead of your own. Holding the leash in your right hand, extend that arm forward and ever so slightly to the right. As you do this, because what you are doing is subtle, the dog will begin to go in the direc-

tion of the pressure. It's so slight, he won't fight it. He hardly knows it's there. Keep the pressure steady, bringing your dog in a lovely, wide circle, around, around until he circles behind you. Swap the leash behind your back into your left hand, and there he is, as if by magic, at your left side in the heel position. He will look

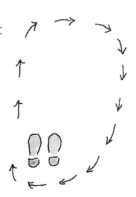

very surprised, not having the faintest idea how he got there. Praise him warmly and continue your walk. When he pulls again—and he will—circle him again and praise him for appearing so neatly at your side.

Some dogs, even big ones, are so gentle and light on their feet, you won't have much of a problem. Other dogs—chunky, big-chested, muscular dogs, dogs so strong they could move mountains and would love to, thank you—tend to pull. Thick-bodied, thick-headed dogs tend to be forgetful, too, or at least single-minded. Even if well trained, when they get a particularly good scent or are on the way to the park they forget the training, they forget your poor arm, they just go. That single-mindedness is exactly what is needed to get a task done—win a weight pull, for example—but on a walk on leash, it can be a handicap (for you). Using the above method and holding tight with both hands to your sense of humor will keep you on good terms with even the most cement-headed dog, and the move is graceful, too. No one watching you in action will ever tell you you're being mean.

Suppose you find that no matter how many times you cause your dog to circle around behind you and end up, at least momentarily, at your left side, he continues to forget himself and pull again? That may be nature's way of telling you that this particular dog needs to learn to heel (see "Walking on the Leash," chapter 7). Some dogs need the structure of heeling, especially on the way out. Most will learn not to pull, even without the "Heel" command, on the way back.

Six

No-Training Training

No-training training is done by and large with tone of voice. The following important commands make living with a dog much safer and easier, yet are so simple to teach that they can be taught without the foundation of basic obedience training.

By now, your dog has learned enough that you should be able to teach these commands in next to no time.

"Watch Me"

When you become alpha to your dog, he will automatically pay more attention to you. He needs to know your intentions, your moods, because they affect him. Moreover, he wants to please you or, at the very least, keep out of trouble. In order to do that, he *has to* pay attention, to see what works and what doesn't.

However, there will be times when your dog's mind is elsewhere and you need his attention quickly: You want to teach him something or ask him to work for you, you want to give a silent signal, you want to help him to focus because he seems stressed. For these occasions, use "Watch me!"

- Ask your dog to sit, and say "Watch me." As you do, point toward one of his ears, then quickly draw your hand up and point toward your eyes. If his eyes follow your hand and look into your eyes, praise. If after a few tries, your dog won't follow your pointer, try snapping your thumb and middle finger beneath the pointer once as you move your hand toward your eyes.

- Try holding a squeak toy up near your face. "Watch me," *squeak, "Good* dog!"

- Some dogs will simply look into your eyes if you merely say "Watch me" or if you whistle, then say it.

Dominant dogs may not want to "give" you their eyes at first. It's giving up something—leadership, the thing they want to keep. Stay with it, and with the training, and they will learn to look to you for direction.

Submissive dogs need time to learn that it is okay to look alpha in the eye. Among dogs, eye-to-eye contact is an aggressive act. If you think about it, it can be among people, too. But it can also be a benign act, an expression of curiosity or attentiveness, even affection. This is the very lesson *pet* dogs need to learn, that eye contact means not one thing, as in the wild, but many things. Because dogs are so adept at reading the content of what is in your eyes, once they learn it's okay to look, the rest is easy for them.

This said, it shouldn't take more than a minute or two to find something that will work, and it should take no time at all to practice this "command" because you can toss in a quick "Watch me" when you are about to feed your dog, put on his leash, even when you pass by him in the house. Of course, use it before teaching a command. It's a way of letting him know you're about to work.

"LEAVE IT"

Does your dog scarf up cigarette butts or chicken bones in the street or steal defrosting steaks from your kitchen counter? "Leave it" is the command you need.

"Leave it" is said with a deep tone of voice. It's serious. Indoors, use it to warn your dog when he's ogling the cheese and crackers set out for guests. Outside, add a pop of the leash to "Leave it" when the dog pulls toward that pizza crust on the sidewalk or the blowing leaf.

Please do remember how different breeds of dogs vary. You can teach a biddable dog "Leave it" with a few tries. But if you have a terrier, it will take many, many, many repetitions for him to take this seriously. He was bred not to give in. So if you have a terrier and a blowing leaf, a steak or crinkly paper in your wastebasket, you're going to need more stick-to-itiveness than he has. A lot. It's not that he's stupid—far from it. He's tough-minded.

TIMESAVING TIPS

Practice "Leave it" by using setups. When you have a few minutes, place a piece of bread on the coffee table, watch and wait. If your dog is faster than a speeding bullet, tie a long string to his collar and hold the other end so that your "Leave it," until he learns it, has more clout.

Now hear this: Do not wait until the bread is passing through your dog's digestive system to say "Leave it." Correct him when he *thinks* about stealing the bread. When he ogles the bread, say "Leave it!" and pop the string. Praise when he looks at you and admires your power. Give him one more try. Then remove the bread and eat or toss it. Never give your dog the thing you just told him to leave. If you do, you're teaching "Wait," which has a whole different application.

Once your dog learns the narrow use of "Leave it," with your help, he will be able to broaden its use. We use "Leave it" to tell Dexter to ignore an approaching dog who looks like trouble. I once used it when he was off leash at the dog run. He had decided to see if a huge intact male dog, an apartment house with teeth, wanted to be his best friend. I didn't have time to get to him before he would have reached the other dog. To my delight and relief, he understood this broader use of "Leave it" and changed his direction, heading for a gentle-looking Brittany instead. Good boy, Dexter!

"WAIT"

"Wait" isn't an essential command, less urgent to teach than "Leave it," but it's easy to teach and it's a nice refinement in your communication with your dog.

"Stay" means freeze. You do not want to tell your dog to stay and then leave the house without breaking the command. If you do, the dog will have to break the command himself. Then he's learning the opposite of what you want to teach him—quit when you feel like it instead of quit when the master says it's okay.

"Wait," on the other hand, means give this a minute. Said at the curb, it means: We'll be moving again in a moment. It means: Don't take this biscuit just yet. It means: Don't rush out the door. It means: Don't leave the car until I say okay. It says: Be patient, everything will change in a moment.

Using two words instead of one allows each to be more specific, more accurate. I take words seriously, so this pleases me immensely. More important, I have seen the effect on dogs I am training. They really *do* understand the difference. "Stay" puts them on guard; "Wait" is a more relaxing command. It's easier. Don't do anything special, it says; there's just a small delay here. Dogs like to know what's going on.

"ON"

"On" is taught with a patting hand. Pat your bed. Say "On." Like magic, there's your dog. Pat the couch, a park bench, your lap.

"On" is an invitation. I never met a dog who didn't get it right off.

"OFF"

"Off" is the opposite of "On." It means get off the couch, get off the bed, get off my lap. "Off" needs a gruffer voice than "On," and with some dogs, it needs a tug of the leash or a hand slipped into a buckle collar and a tug. As you might imagine, "Off" will come in handy and is well worth the few minutes it will take to teach it.

A word of caution is in order here. Your Golden Retriever, born to please you, will respond more quickly to "Off" than your Basenji, born to please himself.

Understanding your dog's breed character and individual personality will help you to predict how easy or difficult teaching any given command will be. A dog with a good sense of humor, for example, like a Poodle or a German Shepherd or a foxy Shiba Inu, may *intentionally* get up on the couch, as a joke, just to get you to say "Off." Whether or not you enjoy the joke may have more to do with the fabric, color and age of your couch than it has to do with anything else. On the other hand, the Shiba, for example, is terrific at static commands. Give him a "Stay" and you've got a bookend. A Golden, a Lab or a Flat-Coated Retriever will heel like a dream and retrieve a ball easily. The Shepherd is a quick study, devoted to his master and, more astoundingly, he understands the world he lives in. Each dog learns different things at different paces and is good at some things, less good at others. By trying many commands, especially these quick ones, you'll begin to really understand your dog.

"Turn Around"

If you bathe your dog at home, in the bathtub, you'll want to teach "Turn around." In the middle of the bath, when you are ready to do his other side, simply pat the far end of the tub, saying "Turn around." If this doesn't get your dog to turn and look, or turn around, gently, as you repeat the command, lead him around and praise him as you do.

We also use "Get in" for the even larger problem of getting a big dog into the tub. Dexter doesn't love a bath, but he will jump into the tub on command. How else would I be able to keep the white white?

We don't fill the tub to bathe a dog. We tell the dog to "Get in" to a dry tub, wet him with a spray, soap him nicely, and rinse him off. This means the tub looks the same on bath days and all other days. Empty.

Teach "Get in" by saying it as you toss in a favorite toy. Your dog will jump into the tub, grab his toy and immediately jump out. Praise like crazy. This is your foundation work. Practice while you brush your teeth, unless you're the only person in the United States whose dog doesn't follow you to the bathroom.

Of course, even with an empty tub, your dog will know when it's bath day, the little psychic. Here's where being alpha makes the command work. Get your dog. Close the bathroom door. Tap the tub. Seriously tell your dog "Get in." Now you're in business. A little song wouldn't hurt, would it? My dog loves his bath song. He's the only one I know who doesn't hold his ears when I sing.

You won't need "Get out." I never met a dog who stayed in the tub after being told "Okay."

"LET'S GO"

What do you say to move a dog who has cemented himself to a scent? You won't say "Heel," not unless you've taught it. You won't say "Come," not unless you want your dog to sit in front of you. When you want your dog to "Move, dammit," you won't say *that*. People will think you're grouchy.

Say "Let's go" in a cheerful, in-charge voice, pop the leash and walk. And don't forget to say "*Good* dog" when he follows right along.

Let's go!

Seven

Essentials

By now your dog is half trained. He's doing better on his end of the leash. You're doing better on yours. Before you begin the next important commands, take a minute to look once again at the fascinating process of his learning.

HOW DOGS *REALLY* LEARN

Late last century, a horse named Hans was purported to have the astonishing ability to solve mathematical problems, consistently tapping out the correct answer with his hoof. For a while, Hans and his owner, Van Osten, were all the rage. But eventually, after many tests

Other animals have been thought to speak, spell or do math.

in which Hans, dubbed Clever Hans, proved himself clever indeed, one Oskar Pfungst, after experiments of his own, published his view that Hans was not doing math at all. What was happening, he claimed, was that the horse was keying in on small unconscious movements of the eyes or head of the experimenter that let him know when he had tapped out the right number. Van Osten, heart-broken and ashamed, died years later in obscurity.

Other animals—horses, and of course dogs as well—have been thought to speak, spell or do math, and each time they were "unmasked," knowledge about animal intelligence took a giant step backward. After all, is the fact that the horse Clever Hans could not actually do mathematical problems the most significant fact that arose in the many studies in which he participated? Isn't what he actually *did* do at least as important?

At that time, it was thought that Hans was responding to an accidental subliminal cue. This means that he was able to pay care-ful enough attention to his human testers that he could notice signs so elusive that for a rather long time, all the human observers missed them. On top of that, he was able to understand that when he saw these subtle cues, the raised eyebrow, the slight tilt of the head, it meant he had reached the tester's goal. Fantastic as that is, having considered the Clever Hans Syndrome while training dogs, I think the truth is even more fantastic. I don't believe it was an outward clue to which Hans responded. I believe he felt the tester's pleasure when the correct number of taps had been made.

Years ago, when I began training dogs professionally, I used to take my Golden Retriever, Oliver, anyplace I'd be invited—libraries, schools, nursing homes, even a mental institution—and do a little talk on dogs, hoping to get myself known in the area in which I worked. The highlight of any show, no matter its purpose, was always one of Ollie's amazing barking tricks.

For adults and older kids, Oliver might, for instance, bark the square root of twenty-five. For little children, we might do two plus two. Ollie *loved* an audience. Because he was so happy and excited when performing, he learned tricks very quickly. First, he figured out that when a question began with the word *how*, as in, "How much is two plus two?" he should bark when I stopped speaking, and keep on going until I petted or praised him. The next stage was that instead of saying, "Good boy," to stop the barking at the "right answer," I would simply break eye contact. The third and most interesting stage was when I no longer had to do anything to let Ollie know that the desired number of barks had been reached. Clever Oliver would pick up from the audience just when it was time to stop and reap his reward, a rush of pleasure followed immediately by applause and laughter. Instead of watching *me* for the signal to stop, he'd pay most careful attention to the children, always stopping at exactly the right number.

I began to watch the children, too, to see what Oliver was seeing. But this happened in many classrooms with many different children. This was not an issue of consistent accidental cueing. Something universal was going on.

It seemed to me that when the "right answer" was achieved, the children would relax, relieved, as it were, that the dog got it right. Next, they became excited and would clap and giggle. Once Oliver keyed in on the kids, my own learning curve took an upward swing. Now it became clear to me that despite what my clients said, for instance, about how upset they were that their dogs stole food, the dogs that continued to steal, even in the face of corrections, did so because they accurately picked up the emotion underneath—pleasure. In those situations where, in truth, owners thought it was adorable, funny and cute that their dogs stole, the dogs were receiving the same sort of positive reinforcement both Hans and Oliver had been clever enough to learn from.

About the time of the school demonstrations, I was also going to a lot of dog shows to observe and learn. This was many years ago, before the flip finish, in which the dog jumps and turns in the air, became a standard alternative for getting a dog back to the heel position. I was admiring a Miniature Poodle working beautifully in

the obedience ring when it came time for the finish.
The little dog executed a perfect flip, but the audience, many of whom knew little of obedience work
and were watching the proceedings for its entertain-
ment value only, laughed. The Poodle, whose attention had been totally on his handler,
turned to face the audience, and
desirous of more of the lovely positive
reinforcement that laughter can give a
dog, hopped, skipped and flipped his
way through the rest of the perfor- When owners find it funny,
mance, blowing his green ribbon for dogs continue to steal.
that performance. It was clear that eliciting pleasure in observers,
whether they are asking mathematical questions or simply watching a performance, is something animals will work for.

Although poor Hans was discounted because he wasn't doing
math, the Clever Hans Syndrome or unintentional training is an
important aspect of understanding dog behavior. It can explain
interesting phenomena, such as how your dog knows not only
when you are about to go out, but whether or not you plan to take
him along. Don't be fooled by supplicating tail wags. Just because a
dog knows the awful truth doesn't mean he'll accept it lying down.
If you have ever tried to convince your dog you were asleep by
merely closing your eyes, you already know this. Most dogs can't be
fooled. Physiological changes, however subtle, tell the animal all
sorts of truths about you, that you are sad or happy, pleased or
annoyed, relaxed or afraid, really sleeping or awake with your eyes
closed—whatever the case may be.

Clever Hans also taught us that accidental cueing can have dangerous results. Take, for example, the aggressive dog whose owner
protests the dog's dangerous behavior but inwardly feels pleased to
be protected. No matter what this owner does, the reinforcement
coming from what he feels, even if those feelings are unconscious, is
far more potent to the dog.

It is by noting and responding to subliminal cues and the physiological changes that accompany emotions that dogs learn much of what is true about their owners and their world, an important lesson we learned from a most clever horse named Hans, and the very lesson that will now help you to quickly teach the essential commands "Heel," "Stay," "Come" and "Down" to your dog.

WALKING ON THE LEASH

You have already done the follow-me game, including the stage where you turn and change direction without enticing the dog to come along. This will keep your dog fairly close and pretty attentive, even before you tighten "Follow me" to "Heel."

Now when you take your dog out on leash, take three minutes in the middle of his walk to work on "Heel." After your dog has had sufficient time to relieve himself, begin as you would for "Follow me," walking one way, then doing an about-face and walking in the opposite direction. If your dog is not paying attention, he will cor-

rect himself when the leash becomes taut. A couple of turns should get him watching.

Now simply up your expectations. Patting your left leg, because heel is traditionally done at the left side, and folding your leash so that there is less slack, introduce the word *heel* as you continue the follow-me game. Once you begin to use the "Heel" command in addition to enticements, your goal is to encourage your dog to stay much closer and to stay at your left.

Proper heeling requires the dog to begin working seated at your left side, in the heel position, and to stop and sit at your left, even with your hip and facing forward, whenever you stop. For now, who cares! We're not going to rush into this. We are going to work three minutes, maybe four, on every walk, just tightening "Follow me" so that the dog now walks along at your left side, turning with you when you turn without having to be cued, reminded or yanked.

Only after the dog is consistently walking at your pace will you add the automatic "Sit," asking the dog to sit when you stop and praising him for doing so.

Expect this new work to take at least a few weeks to gel. Go back to the old "Follow me" game anytime you feel you've gone too fast, and, when you're ready, reel your dog in, tapping your leg, telling him he's handsome, praising him warmly when he trots nicely at your side.

What if he darts ahead and pulls? Simply extend your right arm with the leash firmly, and gently move arm and leash to the right until your dog begins to circle. Then lead him in a great, wide circle around behind you, swapping hands on the leash, until your surprised dog ends up at your left in the heel position. Tell him he's the smartest dog ever born. Tap your leg and go, go, go.

TIMESAVING TIP

It is much easier for your dog to heel at a quick pace than a slow one. Walking slowly gives your dog time to get distracted. He will already have had a good chance to relieve himself, and he will get another chance to do so after his three-minute training session. So it is surely humane to ask him to do nothing at all except to walk along at your side for three minutes.

Walking slowly also may make it appear to your dog that you are waiting for him. This is appropriate when he is relieving himself, or when you are giving him time to sniff, but *not* when you are heeling. You are in charge. You set the pace—fast while you're teaching, then any pace you like once your dog is trained to heel.

STAYING PUT

Now that you have some foundation work done, it's time to add "Stay" to your dog's nice "Sit."

With your dog on leash, ask him to sit. Hold the leash folded, so that it is taut, not tight, and stand near your dog, no more than one step away. Swing your flat, open hand, palm facing your dog, toward your dog's nose, stopping two inches in front of it, saying "Sta-a-y." Stand. Don't sit or crouch. If you get smaller, your dog will break faster. Now wait. Your dog will break. Count on it.

Some of my clients shrug their shoulders when their dogs break. They look at me and say, "See!"

That's not terrifically productive. Instead, put your dog exactly where he started, as if there were an X taped on the floor, tell him "Sit," tell him "Stay," count three chimpanzees and tell him

"Okay." Let him approach for his praise, and try only once more during this session.

Suppose your dog breaks in one chimpanzee? Then correct him as above, returning him to the same spot, and try again. In less than ten minutes, you should be able to get one or two short "Sit/stays." Bravo to you both. Practice again tomorrow.

TIMESAVING TIP

If you work on "Sit/stay" *after* your dog's adventure walk, he will be ten times easier to train than if you try this static command when your dog is bursting with energy and bouncing off the ceiling. Teaching quiet commands when your dog is tired is not cheating; it's brilliant dog training, if I must say so myself. After your dog understands what you want, practice by using "Stay" when you need it, on leash, please.

Some people think that if a little is good, a lot is better. Not me. I prefer not to push an untrained dog to work for more than a few minutes at a time. Worked for too long, the quality of the dog's work and his ability to concentrate will both diminish.

When I have a private lesson with a dog and his master, that lesson lasts considerably more than ten minutes. But, indoors or out, the work is broken up into five- and ten-minute segments. Sometimes the dog is just allowed to sniff and walk along on a loose lead.

Sometimes my dog Dexter comes along on the lesson, to work and play with my client's dog. In this case, the dogs work together, then play, then work, then play. This keeps the lesson lively and prevents the dog who is learning new things from becoming stressed or burned out.

In time, of course, as your dog's work improves and as he matures, he will be able to concentrate and work for longer periods of time.

COMING WHEN CALLED

When you want your dog to come to you from a distance, small or vast, you want to project the message that you are friendly. This will make him run to you.

- Beginning at home, indoors, using your new "Sit/stay," put your dog on command, walk to the end of his leash, crouch, put your arms out to the side and sweetly call your dog. When he comes, fold your arms around him in a quick hug, tell him he's fabulous, stand, walk him to another spot and try again.

- When your dog is not on leash, not on a "Sit/stay" and not right next to you but within your sight, crouch and call him to come. Praise. Toss a toy for him.

- When you play fetch with your dog, toss the toy, telling him "Take it!" If it is his habit to return to you with the toy, use this game to practice "Come."

- If you have a fenced yard, practice "Come" in the yard, first on leash, then off leash.

- When you are about to offer your dog something that will make him come running, like dinner, a walk or his favorite toy, call him to come, thus practicing this important command by using it when you are sure it will be successful.

- Always praise your dog for coming.

- Never call your dog for punishment.

- Always *entice* the dog who is reluctant to come. Squeak a toy. Hide a toy and squeak it. Cover your face and call your dog. Cover your face and whine like a puppy. If none of these work, go back to working on leash and patiently start again.

- When you know for sure your dog won't come, don't call him. If you do, he learns he does not have to listen to the command "Come." If he won't come because, let's say, he's busy playing with another dog, and it's time to go, go and get him.

- Do not take your dog off leash in an unfenced area. Dogs always know when they are "free." They know the difference between a fenced place and an unfenced place. In addition, your young pup may be reliable, attached to you, not bold enough to run off, but when adolescence hits, he'll be full of himself, experimental, even bratty. The dog who wouldn't stray at four months might head for God-knows-where at nine or ten months. Do not take chances with your dog.

What if all you want is an off-leash come? My suggestion is that you take your dog to class. *Reliable* off-leash work takes lots of time. In class, under the guidance of a professional trainer, your dog will learn to come when called even with the temptation of other dogs close by. Once he does well in an off-leash class, you may want to try him in outdoor, fenced areas, and if that goes well, safe, unfenced areas, such as your local park.

Please don't kid yourself when it comes to your dog's safety. If your dog does not come reliably in a fenced area, don't think he'll do better at the park. Also, be aware that no matter how well trained your dog is, taking him off leash out-of-doors where there is no fence is a risk. You may feel, after lots of training, that the risk is minimal. On the other hand, if your dog is a runner, even if he comes reliably in class, once free to run, he is likely to do so.

Any training you do with your dog will improve your chances of getting him to come when you call him because training tightens the bond between you and your pet. Still, caution is advised.

LYING DOWN

"Down" is a tricky command to teach because it asks the dog to assume a submissive posture. Because most puppies and preadolescents do this easily and naturally, even rolling onto their backs for a belly rub, youth is the easiest time to teach this command. Once a dog is an adolescent, and in that *how larger than life am I* frame of mind, or an adult, it is more difficult, at first, to get an amiable response when teaching "Down." But because it is a submissive posture, and because having your dog lie down on command is a clear, benign reminder that you, not he, are top dog, you really need to teach it.

Here are some tips before you begin.

- Teach the "Down" command as it comes up in this book, after teaching many other commands. This way, your dog already knows you are in charge. This makes the "Down" command more acceptable to him. Teach "Down" slowly, working a minute or two at a time. Don't keep pressing your dog. Don't rush the teaching.

- Teach "Down" indoors with no other dogs present. Your male will feel he's losing face to assume a submissive posture in front of another male dog, even if it's your own. Once he knows the command, you can use it as you need it.

- Most important, until your dog lies down on command without a fuss, do these lessons *after* his exercise, preferably when he's pooped. Cheating? Smart!

If your pet is still a pup, ask him to sit, pat the floor in front of him with one hand, then scoop up his front legs, lifting them a little higher than you would have to in order to bring them forward, then bring them forward, slowly, and place them back on the floor. Work on a carpet. Speak gently. Encourage your dog to roll over for a belly rub. This makes the "Down" command appealing and benign.

Some young dogs will learn this easily. Others won't. If yours won't, try a toy as a lure. With your dog on a "Sit/stay," pat the floor, saying "Down," and bring the toy in an L pattern, straight down in front of him, then along the floor, stopping where his paws will be when he lies down to get it.

Gently lift...   ...and gently place. Good Annie!

Once I was training an inscrutable Chow Chow, an intact male adult. He was so touchy I had to train him as if he were a puppy, with gentle, tiny tugs on the leash and a soft voice. But once I did that, he learned in a flash, heeling as slowly as his mistress, who walked with a cane, the very first day. However, when we got to the "Down" command, he growled. He had never been aggressive to me. In fact, he had never shown *any* emotion. Most of the time, he was like a statue of a dog—until I asked him to assume the position. Had I pressed him, I might have gotten bitten. In addition, his mistress, whose leg had been broken in a fall, could not press him. So what was the point? Instead, knowing once I asked him to lie down I best get him to do it or he'd learn he didn't have to listen to me or his mistress, I asked for his favorite toy. I was handed a tennis ball. At the sight of it, the growly Chow changed his demeanor. He became an enthusiastic puppy. I asked him to sit. Eyes on the ball, he did so. Then I repeated the "Down" command, making an L with the ball, and he pounced into the "Down" position, getting the ball as a reward. Happily, he did this each time he was asked, for me as well as for his owner. In time, he obeyed the command without the lure *or* the growl. May you be so lucky.

Suppose your Chow or Smooth Fox Terrier or Springer Spaniel won't lie down for a toy. Then what? If *your* dog is aggressive, this is the time to get professional help. If not, and the above methods have not done the trick, try a surprise. With your dog on a "Sit/stay," signal "Down," then swiftly grasp his buckle collar and the foreleg on your side. Now, at once, pull the collar toward you and lift the leg, lying your dog down onto his side. Praise well, then release the dog with an "Okay." After a week or so of practice, once or twice a day, work on "Down/stay" as you did "Sit/stay."

TIMESAVING TIP

When educating your dog, particularly when teaching "Down," slower is faster. Working slowly gives the dog a chance to absorb the lesson. Quick results can be impermanent. Even if you have all the time in the world, teaching your dog for a few minutes at a time makes good sense.

A PICTIONARY OF HAND SIGNALS

"Sit"

"Stay"

"Down"

"Heel"

"Come"

PART THREE

Anticipation

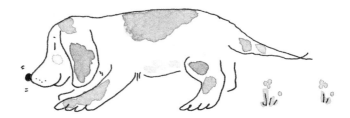

Eight

Life Insurance

The best way to deal with trouble is to try to prevent it, pray it won't happen and, just in case, prepare in advance for its eventuality. Anticipating problems before they occur means that the skills you and your dog might need for your safety and his will be in place, should you ever need them. After all, it's too late to teach your dog to bark on a hand signal when the burglar is already lurking outside your door. Preparation for that possibility should be done right now.

"SPEAK"

Unless you have a Basenji, the barkless dog of Africa, your dog probably barks. We are going to take advantage of him now by putting his barking on cue.

You know better than anyone what makes your dog bark now—a rap at the door, the sound of the telephone, watching you eat something he feels he should be eating, the sight of a squirrel in the backyard, the arrival of guests or, far more exciting, a person in uniform. Before you begin teaching "Speak," simply note what triggers barking in your dog and use that sight or sound.

Let's say your dog barks at the door. Fine. Tell him "Speak" and rap on the door or ring your bell. If you want to get fancy, ask someone else to knock or ring, but it usually isn't necessary. The response to the door is usually so automatic in dogs that even if they see you doing it, they'll still bark.

So, say "Speak," knock, praise for the bark.

Use any other trigger you observe, working less than a minute at a time, whenever you are able.

Soon enough, your dog will bark when you say "Speak." Praise him. And now add a hand signal, tapping your thumb with your pointer as if your fingers were a little, barking mouth.

Why a hand signal?

Suppose one day you hear a prowler outside your door or window. If you say "Speak," who will be afraid of your trick dog? But if you silently signal your dog to bark, you can say anything you like. You can say, "Who's there? Watch him!" You can scare the prowler away.

Now that you're in better shape, it's time for some insurance to protect your dog.

"SMELL IT"

"Smell it" takes nowhere near ten minutes to teach. It's almost instant.

Collect ten items. Anything will do—a lipstick, a comb, a wallet, a bookend, a book, a shoe, a tissue, eyeglasses, a spoon, a pencil, and so on.

Call your dog, ask him to sit and, one at a time, present him with the objects, holding them up for him to sniff, saying "Smell it, good dog, smell it."

Because dogs use their noses the way people use their eyes, as the prime sense, a dog

will smell anything you offer him. Praise for each sniff. Then practice in passing, anytime you think of it and have something in your hand.

"Smell it, good dog!"

"Smell it" is insurance against fear. Dogs go through two fear periods: one in early puppyhood, about eight to ten weeks of age, and the other during adolescence, between eight and ten months of age. During adolescence, when a dog gets frightened of a strange object, he may refuse to walk, back out of his collar and hold tight to the fear for a lifetime. Leaving the dog where he is, at

Never let your dog bolt and run.

the end of his leash, tap the overturned trash can, the open umbrella or the box UPS has just delivered, saying, "Smell it, good dog, smell it." Never let your dog bolt and run. Instead give him all the time he needs to slink up to the "monster" and sniff. Once he does, he'll know immediately that the trash can, umbrella or box is harmless. Praise like crazy for his bravery.

Insurance: It can help your dog overcome fear.

"Find Me"

Okay, let's suppose you read all my cautions and caveats about having your dog off leash and you did it anyway. Or suppose someone left the front door open and, whoops, he got out.

Suppose you see your dog, you call him, but he just won't come.

You try crouching, arms out to the sides. Nothing.

You could cover your face and whine like a puppy. Curiosity has worked in the past. But not today.

Your dog is in danger. What do you do?

Before it happens, like today, teach "Find me." Starting indoors, even when your dog is not fully grown, tell him "Find me" and run away. Then turn, crouch and let him pounce. Tell him he's great and try it again.

As your dog gets hooked on this silly game, up the stakes. Put him on a "Sit/stay." Hide in another room. Call out "Find me." Praise like crazy when he does.

Now hide in the closet, the door ajar. "Find me!"

You're having fun. Your dog is having fun. But it's insurance. Now you're outside. So is your dog. Someone left the door unlatched or his leash snapped. You see him, but he's playing keep-away. In a cheerful, playful voice, tell him "Find me, find me," and turn and begin to run away from your dog. Get behind a tree and crouch. And since this *is* an emergency, prayer wouldn't hurt either.

Many dogs, knowing "Come" means "the fun is over," may ignore "Come" when they are free. But I have seen many a dog tricked into coming with the "Find me" game.

THE EMERGENCY SIT

Here's another life insurance policy. The sit. Your dog is taking off. He won't come when called. He won't even turn and look at you, not even to thumb his nose. Call his name and then say "Sit." Say it commandingly, seriously, authoritatively. He is more likely to sit than to turn and come and, once he does, he's yours. You can add "Stay" or "Wait," then calmly go up to your dog and snap on his leash. Proceed casually. If you run toward your dog or shout, you might scare him off.

You can even try *the emergency sit* followed by "Come." Once your dog has obeyed you, he's more likely to do it a second time.

No dog is fully insured against accident or disaster. Life is neither so simple, nor so kind. But each trick you have up your sleeve to retrieve a runaway increases your chances of safeguarding the dog you love.

Nine

How to De-Stress
Your Dog

D o you run, go to a gym, practice t'ai chi, do yoga? If so, you know that constructive use of the mind and body helps you to shed stress and tension.

Dogs become stressed, too. In fact, dogs not only become tense and edgy from things that stress them directly—being left alone, the presence of an aggressive dog, a huge upset in their routine—but they also absorb our stress. When you are nervous, tense, overtired, unhappy, angry or blue, your dog will soak up those bad feelings as if he were a sponge. The best way to help him get rid of stress and feel good again is to take him to the park, where he can play with other friendly dogs or just run around and enjoy being a dog.

You can also help yourself and your dog de-stress at home, in quiet ways. One way is to brush him, sitting on the floor, perhaps with your favorite music playing or even something you like on television. Brush your dog head to tail, pulling the energy from one end to the other in long, smooth strokes. You can even alternate the brush and your hand, brush, stroke, brush, stroke, until your hand

79

gets warm and you and your dog feel mellow. It won't take more than ten minutes of your time.

If you feel tense or your dog feels tense and you don't have a brush with you, do the above "brushing" with your hands, one after the other, long strokes from the top of your dog's head right to the tip of his tail.

You can get fancier if you like, adding massage to your relaxation session. In between those long strokes down your dog's back, stop and knead the muscles of his neck, working your fingers in small circles behind each ear, down the back of the neck, then along each side of the spine.

If your dog is injured, if he's pulled a muscle or if he has bad hips or elbows, you can gently massage the area that hurts him, bringing warmth via your hands to his injured spot. The massage will increase blood flow and help your dog to heal. But it will also calm him and make you feel kind and useful.

Work can help your dog de-stress. When stress causes him to lose his focus and feel confused, a lively session of heeling with a couple of "Sit/stays" and recalls added in, accompanied by lots of praise, can bring him back to his mellow self. This is not the time to teach something new. That adds stress. Instead, use work your dog has already mastered to remind him that you are in charge and

Steve and I talked about taking Dexter along...

that there is order in his world, a message that will help to diminish his stress.

The premier relaxer may be swimming, which can wash the stress right out of your dog in nearly no time. If you live near a pond, river, lake or ocean, take your dog for a swim whenever weather permits and you have the time. Or if, like me, you are an admitted and practicing dogaholic, you might even take your dog along on a vacation where you can swim together.

My husband Steve and I love to take vacations with our dog, so much so that we've even talked about one day taking Dexter along to Italy or France, where dogs are welcome nearly everywhere.

On our most recent vacation, a trip to England, where quarantine laws made the decision for us, I missed Dexter much too much. Several times while away I woke up with my heart pounding. Had I been at home, I would have simply gotten in close proximity to my dog. Doing so, I tend to quickly adopt his breathing pattern and in a moment I am calm. There, all I could do was wait, feeling the oting the lack of Dexter's presence causes me and wishing only to be home. For me, being away is wonderful, but no country can match up to any place I happen to be in the company of the dog I love.

Now there's scientific support for what I've known all my life to be true, that just being near a beloved pet makes you feel better.

Studies have shown that the presence of a pet lowers the owner's blood pressure and deepens respiration. Your pulse rate goes down. You stop hyperventilating. Your self-esteem becomes elevated, but not enough to make you act like a fool. And, miraculously, the very same physiological occurrences happen to your dog. Simply being together, hanging out, helps you and your dog both to shed the stress we all accumulate just by living.

Ten

Ten Secrets of Problem Correction

T here are two kinds of dog problems. The first, growing-up problems, are covered in this book. These are not really problems. Every dog needs to learn how to live with his human family, how to act in a civilized manner, play without biting, relieve himself out-of-doors and obey a few commands for safety's sake.

House training, therefore, should be considered an expected part of every dog's education, not a problem. Pulling isn't a problem either. It is merely a signal that the dog has not yet been taught to heel. Even wildness isn't a problem. It is either a temporary side effect of adolescence or a symptom of too little exercise.

A problem dog is a dog who destroys your home when left alone, even after puppyhood, a dog who bullies, a dog who bites. A fearful dog can be a problem, especially if the fear inspires him to defend himself. Even a dog who seems to be overly in love with the sound of his own voice may be a problem, unless you live in the woods.

If you have taught your dog the lessons described in this book but your dog is still a problem, more than likely you will need the advice and support of a professional dog trainer who can get to know your individual dog and set up a rehabilitation program expressly for him. Although the following guidelines are too brief to be considered a primer on problem correction (for that, see *Dog Problems* by Carol Lea Benjamin, Howell, 1989), they will still help because they represent the common and uncommon sense you'll need to correct existing problems and prevent new ones from occurring.

When I was a little kid, no one ever hired a dog trainer. In the morning, after breakfast, we opened the door and let the dog out. In the evening, before dinner, someone would stand out front and call the dog to come home. In between, we might meet up with him as he checked out the neighborhood and visited his friends. Sometimes he'd follow our bikes as we rode to the beach. Other times he'd be too busy. There was much less traffic back then, and we lived on a dead-end street. Still, one of our dogs was hit by a car and killed.

It wasn't a great system. But it was what everyone did. Now we know better. Now we know that we are responsible for the safety of our pets, and that includes providing a secure way for them to exercise, not letting them run loose. Now we know that dogs are thinking beings and love a chance to use their minds. Now we know, too, that if help is needed, it is available. Professionals abound who can teach us how to correct the disturbing or dangerous behavior that sometimes spoils the fun of living with a dog or two. People teach seminars and dog obedience classes now, give private training consultations in the home, even write books. If you need help, it's there. Take advantage of it. Although the occasional dog is beyond repair, with a little work, most hooligans can become model canine citizens. In the meanwhile, the following secrets are yours to use. In many cases, they are all you'll need to keep things copacetic in your mixed-species family.

1. DON'T BE AFRAID TO SAY NO.

The word *no* is out of fashion. In our current everyone-is-a-victim culture, people want everything to be "positive" or "nice." It always amazes me to watch otherwise intelligent humans allow their pet dogs to do things they'd never allow another human being to do—urinate in the living room, walk all over the furniture, steal food off of their plates, tug on and even tear their clothes, mouth off nonstop while they are speaking, bite them. I can never figure out why they don't just say no.

In a world full of danger, in a family where others, not just the dog, have rights, this is unrealistic. Balanced with all the caring and fun things you do with your dog, the word *no* is not only a perfectly fine part of your communication with your dog, it's a necessary part. *It will not damage your dog's psyche if he can't get his way every minute.* Saying no is part of the way you communicate your standards, house rules, even your feelings, to your dog. There is nothing wrong with saying no. It can help you to raise a sound, healthy, appropriate dog. And amen to that.

2. If your dog is aggressive, keep him moving.

Aggression, as we have said, is linked to tension. Movement can help your dog blow off the tension he's feeling. So if your dog gets uptight, growly, stiff or still, get him outside and move him around. Run with him, heel him, do some quick recalls, take a hike, toss a ball, have him retrieve a stick.

Was it a temporary glitch, such as the presence of another dog, that made your dog tense? Then moving him elsewhere will do the trick. Was it your attempt to gain the upper hand that did it, such as asking your dog, God forbid, to obey a command? In that case, take your dog to obedience school or call in a trainer with a good reputation who will help your dog understand the appropriate hierarchy for your family.

3. Have your dog work for petting.

If your dog is a problem dog, or you anticipate that he's on the way to becoming one—he's too cheeky, rude, disobedient, bossy or stubborn—don't give in every time he insists you pet him.

In a pack, only the leader gets adoration on demand. Perhaps the constant reassurance your dog asks for is reassurance that he's top dog. In that case, when he comes and puts a paw on your thigh or puts his fine, big head under your hand, ask him to sit, ask him to lie down, ask him to retrieve a toy and only *after* he has obeyed should you pet him. Don't do it for ages, either. If he's a problem, don't prolong the petting sessions until after your dog's behavior has improved.

4. MAKE SURE YOUR EXPECTATIONS ARE APPROPRIATE.

Before I became a dog trainer, I would have guessed that most people expected too much of their dogs. This happens, of course. A young dog is given run of the house. A beginning student is expected to work off leash when he barely does his commands on leash. A pup is expected to wait too many hours between walks.

More often, I have found, people expect too little of their dogs. They fail to get what they are after—instant Lassie—and so think their dogs are dumb. They give up without really trying.

If you have some sort of problem, or don't want one, you need to examine your expectations. Perhaps sometimes they are too high, other times too low. That is, you expect your untrained dog to come when called, but you haven't taught him to do so because you thought he wasn't capable of learning.

I always have high hopes but take small steps in order to get where I want to go. That is, I have short- and long-term goals, and I edit my expectations as my dog learns, matures and catches on. Expecting more, but being realistic, can help you help your dog become the very best, smartest dog he is capable of being.

5. Always begin and end a training session with something your dog does well.

Old-fashioned common sense dictates that when training sessions start and end with something your dog does easily and well, for which he earns praise, both teacher and student will feel enthusiastic about lessons to come. So when you are struggling with the "Down/stay" and your ten-minute session is almost over, end with a cheerful recall, a nifty minute of heeling and lots of praise. It will help you both get back to work next time.

6. Use the silent treatment.

The silent treatment isn't the cold shoulder. Once a week, practice everything your dog knows with hand signals only. It will force your dog to pay attention. It will really make him think. At the end of ten minutes of working this way, your dog will seem hours and hours better trained.

Working quietly is peaceful, too. You'll both like it.

7. Use it or lose it.

If you never practice what you have taught your dog, he'll forget it. So if you have use for the commands you have taught, review them once in a while to keep them sharp.

Use it or lose it is also true about your dog's socialization. He needs to mix with people of all ages and with other nice dogs so that he maintains his social skills.

You'll need to groom him regularly in order for him to accept necessary nail clipping, ear cleaning, dental care and brushing with equanimity. And no, that wasn't a joke—

busy or not, you should be brushing your dog's teeth. It only takes a minute.

Tricks and games are coming your way in the next chapter. If you enjoy them, as your dog surely will, practice, practice, in order not to lose them. Fold one or two into your dog's walks, leave time for a game after dinner and end the evening with a bark, a roll over and a kiss. Why lose a good thing?

8. Do not give your dog more freedom than he can handle.

If you *know* your dog tends to be destructive when left alone, don't give him run of the house. If his house training still slips and slides, use a crate when you have to. If he's a thief, don't leave him alone with your steak.

When it comes to giving your dog freedom, proceed slowly, monitoring his run of your castle when you are able to and keeping him in a puppyproof place when there's no one to watch over him. Eventually, with training and time, he should be a reliable fellow, able to nap anywhere in the house without causing damage.

9. Do not share your bed with a problem dog.

Sleeping *with* you, on the same surface, implies equality. The dog who feels he is your equal is less than a day away from feeling *sure* he's your superior. He's a pack animal. Without clear leadership he assumes there's a job opening, and this sort of equal opportunity employment does not bode well in a mixed-species household.

It's a real plus for your dog if he can sleep in your room. As a pack animal, he craves companionship. But sharing sleeping space makes many a dog bossy. This is something you don't need. Your dog should have his own mat or bed. And he should use it. However, if your dog is not aggressive, and you want to *invite* him up on the bed to cuddle sometimes, there's no harm in doing so. But be sure you can evict him without an argument when it's time for lights out.

10. IF YOUR DOG HAS A PROBLEM, INCREASE HIS EXERCISE.

It is rare to find a problem dog who is getting enough exercise. Here's an obvious fact: A tired dog is a good dog. So if you are having a problem of any kind, figure your dog isn't getting enough exercise. If your dynamo doesn't get the opportunity to use his energy in a constructive way, he's apt to use it destructively.

As you have seen by now, you *can* educate your dog quite well using ten-minute lessons. But ten minutes will not do the trick when it comes to exercise. Unless you have a little peanut who can get pooped running around the house, someone will have to get your dog out for a swim, a run or a romp in the park every day. In addition to your dog's outdoor exercise, you can use the tricks and games coming up next to exercise both his mind and body, indoors or out. As you will soon see, some of these can even be done while you also do other things.

PART FOUR

Recreation

Eleven

Ten Ways to Play

Tricks and games may be selected for your dog by considering his body type, level of energy and individual sense of humor. The more closely you match the trick to the dog, the faster the teaching will proceed. So if you are seriously tight on time, teach your Malamute to howl, your Fox Terrier to jump, your Golden Retriever to sneeze, your Basenji to chortle. Going with the grain is a perfectly valid way to teach tricks.

On the other hand, you may want to teach your dog a particular trick or game because you like it. This, too, is a fine way to select tricks. Any of the tricks here can be taught to any dog. Even a low-slung, long-backed dog can do a jumping trick, as long as the height of the jump is really minimal.

You can also select tricks for your dog by noting what he likes to do on his own. Does he roll over when he's happy? Dexter does. Then mightn't he be happy when you ask him to roll over on command, and reward him for doing so? Dexter is!

Does your dog like to make noise? Howl with him. Or teach him to close a door with a nice, resounding slam. Dexter loves both of these tricks, too.

Is your dog responsive to your moods, attentive and well focused on you? Then sneeze is your trick.

Or simply start at the top and work your way down. Now that you know how easy it is to educate your dog and also how much fun it is, you'll probably want to teach them all, but do so one at a time, please.

1. HOWL

Years ago, I read and heard much about why dogs howl, but differing opinions left me feeling confused. Since I have learned that imitation can begin at the surface, with what one sees and hears, the way children imitate the actions of adults without understanding their significance and proceed to an inner place of understanding, I decided to actually do what I wanted to understand.

At the time, I had a German Shepherd, Scarlet, and I sat near her and began to howl. Shepherds are natural howlers, so she quickly joined in. Ever after, all I had to do to get her to howl with me was to begin to howl. If we were not in the same room when I began, she'd rush to find me, howling as she came.

The fact that you "teach" a dog to howl by howling will give you one of the functions of howling. It is a verbal affirmation of the bond within a community. It works when you are physically close—"We are here, we are here"—or far apart—"I am here, where are you?"

Any breed of dog can be encouraged to do some version of the howl. Some will yip, or bark and howl intermittently. But in each case, the head will tilt up and the dog's mouth will make the characteristic circle of a wolf howling at the moon.

The mournful sound of the howl reverberates in the chest, expressing the emotions of the heart, grief, longing, affection, camaraderie, all woven together in the fabric of a song. In order to not only see but to feel what your dog is feeling, sit near him and howl. If he is not a natural howler, it may take some time and patience. But in less than ten minutes, he will howl with you. Each time you try, his eloquent song will join yours more quickly.

2. Jump, Three Ways

Most dogs love to jump onto things, over things and even, after an initial introduction, through things. For any dog with a healthy back and legs, jumping modest heights can be terrific exercise as well as a very satisfying activity. Here are three jumping games to try.

Jump over Legs

With a stash of your dog's favorite toys hidden on your person, sit on the floor and put your legs on a low barrier, such as a coffee table. (If your dog is very short or very young, simply sit with your legs on the floor and your feet against a wall.) With your dog on one side of your legs, whichever side he happens to be on, toss one of the toys over your legs to the other side, giving him your play-retrieving command if you have one.

Most dogs will walk or jump over a low barrier—in this case, your legs—to get a favorite toy. If not, try the following: If your legs were up on the coffee table, lower them to the floor; next, tease your dog with the toy, just for a couple of seconds, so that it seems more desirable, then toss it again.

In no time, your dog should be jumping over your legs to fetch a toy. Instead of trying to get the toy back and having a struggle, get your dog's attention with the next toy or ball and try again.

With practice—a minute here, a minute or two there—your dog will fetch over your legs and return the toy so that he can do it again. Be sure to keep your dog's size and age in mind; young dogs and short-legged dogs shouldn't be asked to jump over more than a few inches; old dogs shouldn't jump at all. As your dog gets better, gradually raise your legs, using the coffee table, then just holding a leg across a doorway. Some dogs, but not all, get so good they'll jump over a leg even when they could easily go around it, a neat trick in anyone's book.

Next, with your dog wearing a buckle collar and a leash, teach him to:

Jump over a Barrier

Set a narrow board, or, for a large dog, a leaf of your dining-room table, across a doorway. Now the only way in or out of that room is over the barrier. With your dog on leash, take the jump with him, using your most cheerful voice and lots of praise. A few sessions later, send your dog over for a toy, and call him back with the toy. After a week or two, send your dog over the jump, just like so. Once he'll do this, you can look for low fences and other safe barriers when out on a walk and you can spice up any of his walks with a little snappy jumping.

You may wonder if teaching your dog to jump over low fences will encourage him to jump your yard fence. In my experience, it will not. There is no dog so foolish that he does not already know he can jump over a barrier. After all, your dog can already sit or lie down, too. You are merely putting a skill on cue.

Now, once again without a leash, teach your dog to:

Jump through a Hula Hoop

If your old hula hoop is still in the basement, you can save ten bucks. If not, many toy stores or five-and-dimes still stock hula hoops. The easiest way to teach your dog to jump through the hoop is to squeeze the hoop into a doorway and call your dog back and forth, with a toy and praise. Once your dog goes through the hoop as it sits on the floor, raise it, an inch at a time, and have him jump through.

If your dog is a terrier or loves to jump even though he isn't, you can free-hold the hoop and have him jump through whenever and wherever you are both in the mood to be silly and active. You can still toss a toy through to get him going. And be sure to move the hoop down or to either side if your dog appears to want to go around or under rather than through.

Jumping is a happy activity, good exercise and a great reward after a session of more serious work.

3. SNEEZE

Sneezing is a back-and-forth game of focus and imitation. Working without distractions so that your dog's attention is yours, simply try small sneezes to get your dog to imitate you. Sneeze and wait. Sneeze and wait. At first, praise any sound your dog makes in response. Once he sneezes back, only praise him for a sneeze. Work a few sneezes at a time. Then once your dog gets it and will respond to a sneeze with a sneeze, you can have a sneeze conversation any time you feel like it—out on a walk, when your dog follows you into the bathroom, during those boring commercial breaks on TV (hit the mute button so that your dog really hears the sneeze). This isn't a life-saving command. It doesn't count as exercise. In fact, it has no socially redeeming qualities at all. Perhaps that's why I like it. It's just pure fun.

There's a much flashier and more difficult trick cued by a sneeze. This one has purpose, too. In this trick, when you sneeze, your dog fetches you a tissue!

Even if your dog is not a natural retriever, he might like to snap a pop-up tissue out of a Kleenex box.

To try this trick, sneeze and, using your dog's play-retrieve command (ours is "Take it"), hold the box of tissues near your dog and wiggle a loosened tissue.

Here's a time-saving secret. Getting your dog to take the tissue is really easy. It feels naughty, so it's fun. It's lively. It makes noise.

It's something to wad up and chew. Hell, if you were a dog, you'd grab that tissue.

The hard part of the trick is getting the dog to give up the tissue, to bring it to you and let it go in your hand. But showing off with this hilarious trick when it was half taught, the easy half of course, I discovered that no one cares if you actually get the tissue. The sight of the dog getting the tissue from the box, cued by a sneeze, is so funny that while the dog prances around the room turning the tissue into confetti, everyone is too busy laughing to wonder about what comes next.

Of course, if you are a purist, you can work patiently, calling your dog to you and telling him "Out" until he learns to deliver a nearly intact tissue to your hand. But I think most people prefer the short, easy, naughty version of this trick. Dexter surely does!

I should warn you, too, that if you do the trick by mechanically anchoring the tissue box with two-sided tape instead of holding it, while you are laughing you will probably hear pop pop pop as your dog, jolly as a Jack Russell, empties the entire box, one tissue at a time.

Note: Dexter does both tricks and never mixes them up. If I sneeze, he sneezes back—unless I'm holding a box of tissues.

4. WAVE "GOOD-BYE"

This trick is so cute and so easy to teach that it can't be legal.

You have taught your dog to give his paw. Ask him to sit and ask for his paw by gesture, lifting your "paw" near his, but when his paw comes up, don't take it. Instead, tell him "Wave good-bye" and, holding your hand palm down instead of up and higher than you would to accept his offered paw, paw the air and "wave" at your dog. Quickly praise. With practice, he will know the difference between these two cute tricks by the position of your hand as well as by what you say.

5. "BACK UP"

When clients ask me how to stop their dog from stealing from the garbage, I always advise them to put the garbage behind closed doors, under the sink or in the pantry. Prevention is excellent dog training and a genuine time-saver.

In order to teach your dog to back up on command, prevent the problems that too much space might create by working in a hallway. Position yourself so that you and your dog are facing each other and the length of the hall is behind him. Now, as you flick the back of your hands in your dog's direction, much in the same way you would shoo a person who was standing too near, begin to walk forward.

Until you try this, the assumption is that your dog will have no choice but to back up. This is not exactly the case. Your dog may back up. He may sit. He may, feeling confused and rejected, turn around and walk away.

Therefore, "Back up," still an easy trick, is taught as follows: Use the small hand signal, flick, flick, telling your dog "Back up, back up" in a friendly, soft voice so that he doesn't think you're angry at him. If he sits or turns around to leave, you must back up and call him to come. This time, try giving the signal, then hold his face gently, cupping him under the muzzle as you back him up a step or two. As soon as he takes a couple of steps backward, you back up, calling him to come in an animated fashion. This will reward his effort and let him know you aren't angry at him.

Work back and forth, getting your dog to back up, then back up quickly and call your dog to come for praise, then quietly, quietly, flick, flick, getting your dog to take a step or two back, then back up and call him for praise. Work no more than one or two minutes at a time, whenever you are in the mood or whenever you find yourself and your dog in the hall.

When your dog responds reliably to the command by moving backward, you can move the trick out of the hall.

You may be wondering why you should teach your dog to back up on command in the first place. Your dog might be about to walk on a wet floor. He might be crowding you when you lie down on the floor to do your crunches. If, like mine, your dog becomes a service dog, you may sometimes need to back him into small spaces when you take him into restaurants or on the bus or train. Or you may need some distance between you when you are playing catch, which is the next game.

6. CATCH, THREE WAYS

Catch is a great game. It's fun to play out in the yard or at the park. It's even better when you are comfortably ensconced on the couch and your dog wants something to do.

Straight Catch

Most dogs take a few days to catch on to catch. When you first throw something at them, they often let it bounce off their heads without any attempt to catch it. Take heart. Your dog will learn how to catch a ball in next to no time.

In order to motivate your dog to catch, take a small piece of dog biscuit, tell him "Watch me," let him see the tidbit, tell him "Catch" and toss the piece of cookie toward him, aiming for his nose. Should he miss, and he probably will, let him find and eat the biscuit. Even praise him as he does. Praising will keep your focus and your dog's on the fact that the biscuit is not the reward. The real reward, as always, is getting praised for pleasing you.

Keep practicing, a minute or two at a time. As you do, note that you are also practicing good time management. In order to play, your dog must sit when told and respond to "Watch me." They are both part of the game.

Once your dog attempts to catch the flying biscuit, tell him "Leave it" when he tries to scarf it down after missing. Now he's got to catch it to eat it. No matter. By now, he's hooked on the game. Within a week, practicing only a minute or two a day, your dog will be catching the piece of dog biscuit just about every time you toss it, so you are both ready to move on to the next stage.

Ball or Toy Catch

Now replace the biscuit with a favorite ball, small, light squeak toy or little stuffed animal. Get your dog's attention. Get that "Sit." Say "Catch!" and toss the toy. (As your training gets more sophisticated, you can ask him to "Come" and bring the toy when you play this game. For now, don't worry about fine points.) Always clap and praise each catch as if it were a big deal. It is to your dog.

Bounce Catch

With your dog sitting and watching you, cup the ball in your hand, palm down, then bounce it toward your dog as if you were playing hit the penny with him. Do not bounce the ball so that it hits your ceiling. Try to bounce it so that it is easy for the dog to catch it. Helping him succeed will build his confidence. Failure will make him quit. It spoils the fun. After a while, you may notice that your clever dog will know which way the ball will be coming by noting the position of your hand in advance of the throw. So in playing this version of the game, he's not only having fun, he's learning how to concentrate and figure things out, too.

7. "PAWS UP"

"Paws up" is sort of a no-trick trick, taught with enthusiasm and sound. Tap the table, tell your dog "Paws up" and praise. Sit on a chair, tell your dog "Paws up" and tap your legs. Praise.

8. "CLOSE THE DOOR"

This is one of Dexter's favorite tricks because he's big and when he "taps" his paws on the closet door, it slams shut with a satisfying thud. Okay, it shakes the house. Good boy!

Open a closet door a crack—an inch or two will do—and tap the outside of the door, saying "Paws up, close the door." With enthusiasm and practice, any dog that knows "Paws up" will learn "Close the door" in very little time. It's a lovely finish for an evening with company. You give your guests their coats, your dog closes the closet door on command. It also works well as a lively, cheerful, loud five seconds in the middle of the workout that will be presented in the next chapter.

9. "Roll Over"

"Roll over" is not only a really flashy trick, it's a trick with a message. When your dog rolls over, he is passing through a submissive posture. So, like "Give your paw," this is a benign reminder of your relative status, that which allows you to protect your dog and which gives him the comfort of being protected. In addition, dogs do roll over when they are happy. Some will even wiggle in the middle to scratch their backs. Rolling over is fast, energetic and jolly, but it will take a bit more time to teach than "Paws up." However, you still only work a maximum of ten minutes at a time.

Teach "Roll over" after your dog is doing "Down" on command. Tell him "Down," tell him you prefer him to Lassie and Benji, kneel next to him and gently roll him over, giving the command as you do. Then let him jump to his feet and praise him enthusiastically. Practice one or two rolls a day.

You can also sneak in the "Roll over" command when you see your dog is about to roll over. Be sure to praise after he rolls, as if he did it on command. This will help him think the whole thing's a grand idea.

Once your dog starts responding to the command so that you don't have to be rolling him over manually, add a hand signal, a circle made with your hand, left or right, whichever way you want him to roll. If you pay attention to the way your dog lies down, you'll see which way to circle. If his feet are on the left side, for example, he will only be able roll to the right easily. In order to roll left, he'd have to readjust his position, which would make this whole endeavor seem more like work than play.

"Roll over" is a lively activity, and cheerful too. Use it as a flashy end to a training session, or when you come in from a walk, before you give your dog his biscuit. It's also great as part of the 10-minute workout (to follow), certifiably adorable and satisfying enough to be repeated several times.

Dexter rolls over. "Good boy!"

10. "Find It"

"Find it" is a truly dog-centered game because it gives your dog a chance to use his fabulous sense of smell. I also like teaching this game to beginning dogs because, in order to play, which they are instantly motivated to do, they have to do a nifty off-leash "Sit/stay." So, once again, more bang for your buck.

Put your dog on a "Sit/stay." Let him sniff but not scarf a dog biscuit, telling him "Smell it." Warn him once with a second "Sta-a-y," place the biscuit a few feet in front of him, count one chimpanzee and tell him "Okay, find it."

Big deal, you're thinking. How could he not find it? It's right in front of his nose.

Exactly. This is the hook. Once he's hooked, as you have seen before, the game gets more interesting.

Suppose, to start, your greased pig won't stay. First he tries to eat the biscuit and the hand. Next he breaks before the biscuit even touches the ground. Easy. Start him on leash. Hold the leash taut, not tight. Palm the biscuit when his mouth opens. Make him stay by using the leash, or better yet, having a spouse, offspring or friend hold the leash, count one chimpanzee and as you tell him "Okay, find it," give him enough slack on the leash to do just that.

I have taught this game to hundreds of dogs, mostly real beginners, and even the lowest sneak thief in the bunch has learned to stay in order to play. Trust me: Dogs love this game.

Inching ahead slowly, as your dog catches on, obeying the rules of the game and waiting for the command before pouncing on the biscuit, begin to ask more of him. First, move the biscuit farther away. When that goes well, place the biscuit just out of sight—behind a chair, in the hall or just beyond a doorway—still easy to find.

As the weeks pass, take the biscuit farther, deeper into the next room, then finally, onto a low shelf or end table, something your dog can reach. If your dog fails to make a find, help him. Walk near where you hid the cookie, encouraging him by saying "Find it, good dog, find it."

Once your dog can find his biscuit in another room, up on the dresser or on the bed, assuming he's tall enough to reach there with a gentle "Paws up," you can begin to have fun and save time using this game.

Instead of or as part of a meal, hide dog biscuits all around the house, sending your trained dog to find them. Even if your dog is in an adjoining room, you'll hear the sniffing and you can call out your encouragement, "Find it, good dog, find it." When you hear the crunching, praise like crazy. And as soon as the crunching stops, repeat "Find it, find another one."

I sometimes hide Dexter's breakfast this way, sitting at my desk and writing letters while he frisks the house. After each success, I send him to find the next treat. But I keep count in order to avoid sending him on a wild goose chase once all the biscuits have been consumed. It's an easy way to give your dog an activity while you actually get something else done.

Years ago I had a little Golden Retriever, Fanny, who on her own escalated the game to finding out-of-place objects. Whenever I was busy getting dressed, cleaning up or making dinner, I'd send Fanny on a "Find it," her way. She'd bring the socks I'd dropped near the bed the night before, a magazine from a chair, a pencil that had rolled under the couch. Fanny would even pick up money and drop it into my hand. She loved to be busy. It made her happy. And for the little bit of work this fine game takes, your dog can be busy too, even as you toss the salad, brush your teeth or watch TV.

Playing with your dog gives him more than exercise for his fertile mind and strong body. It gives him contact, time with you and fun. And it will remind you, each time you play, even if it's only for a few minutes, why you got a dog in the first place.

Twelve

The 10-Minute Workout

T he 10-minute workout is a dog-comforting routine to do before leaving your dog alone. Though it may be part of your dog's exercise program, especially on your extra-busy days, ten minutes is not enough of a workout for the average, full-of-beans, healthy dog. However, the 10-minute workout can do an astonishing amount for your dog. It can:

- remind your dog of the natural order of his universe

- calm your dog

- challenge your dog's mind and exercise his body

- satisfy your dog's need for your attention

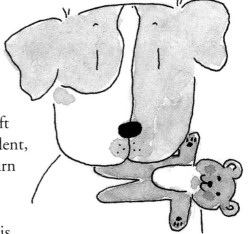

- help ward off separation anxiety

- let your dog know you left on purpose, not by accident, which means you will return

And if you need more good news, the workout is

113

designed to be done while you are getting ready to leave. At some point—and this will differ depending on your dog's age—your dog will get a walk to relieve himself. This is an important part of the message you want to give him, that he has not been forgotten and that you will attend to his needs. Because the walk may be done immediately with a young pup and right before you leave with a grown dog, it is not included in the routine. Here, for starters, is how I do Dexter's workout, which is done after his walk and, even though I work at home, before I "go" to work.

I go to the kitchen to put the kettle on. Dexter follows me. I walk out of the kitchen (ours is small) into the dining area. I open the closet door and ask my dog to close it. Dexter slams it shut, which makes him very happy. If I was only half awake, now I am fully awake. This is a good thing.

I ask Dexter to sit. He sits. I ask him to speak. He barks. I tell him he's the smartest dog ever born.

I pick up a ball or a little teddy bear with a squeaker in it, tell him "Catch" and toss it into his mouth. The water is boiling. I put a tea bag into a cup and pour in the water. Dexter barks again, meaning he wants more attention. He's spoiled. Who cares? Not me. I'm the one who did it.

While the tea steeps, I howl. Dexter howls with me. We both feel connected and wonderful. I finish making the tea, take a few dog biscuits and, carrying the tea toward my desk, I tell Dexter to "Sit," "Stay," then "Smell it." He's psyched. I hide the biscuits all over the apartment: one on the dresser, one on the couch in my office, one on a waist-high cabinet, one in his bed. I tell Dexter "Find it." He begins to frisk the house, looking for a dog biscuit he would reject if I merely handed it to him. He has to work for it, he wants it!

I sit at my desk, wonder who I can call so I won't have to start writing, and say, "Find it, good boy" every once in a while. When I hear crunching, I say, "Good dog." I decide to pay some bills before I write.

I can hear Dexter sniffing in another room, his nose scanning the house. I pay the phone bill. (If I worked away from home, I might be putting on my makeup, looking for panty hose without a run or checking my briefcase to make sure I had whatever I needed for the day.) I hear crunching. I say, "Good dog." Reluctantly, I turn on my computer. This signals me that it's time to write and it lets my dog know it's time for his nap.

Some days, I sit on the floor, prop my heels up on the coffee table and, tossing a toy one way, then the next, send my dog jumping over my legs to retrieve the toy. If you work away from home and dress up, you probably will want to do this one before you suit up. You can do it in your underwear. I never met a dog who'd care one way or the other.

Some days, I might run Dexter through his commands, quickly, with lots of praise: "Hey, good boy, Sit, Stay, Down, Come, that's my genius, Sit, Stay, Catch it, good boy!" Or we may do all tricks: "Speak, Roll over, Find it, Catch, Jump," and so forth.

The 10-minute routine may not even take ten minutes. Frankly, I've never timed it. Sometimes, you may do two minutes' worth, check your watch and simply have to run. Other times, you may get so into relating with your dog, and he may be so sharp and responsive that day, that twenty minutes go by and you're still hiding biscuits or toys or getting jumped over and laughing your head off.

When Dexter was a tiny puppy, we did little routines whenever he woke up, to stimulate his mind, train his eye and strengthen his muscles. (Sometimes I think we overdid it.) For new puppies, the routine should always start with following games.

Pad to the kitchen for tea or coffee; encourage the puppy to follow you. Puppies will get distracted and forget where they are going. No problem; squeak a toy, clap your hands, whistle, call "Puppy, puppy" and he'll be reminded. When you get halfway there, turn, bend and let the puppy catch up. Kiss him. Pet him. Whisper in his ear that he's brilliant and have him continue to follow you. After you fetch your caffeine, have the puppy follow you back to the bedroom so that you can get dressed. Call the puppy and when he comes give him a squeak toy or a chew toy. If he's real-

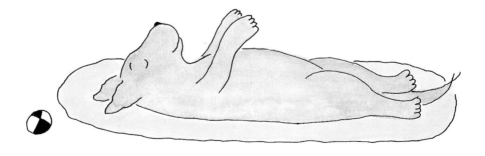

ly young, paper him now, because the stimulation of following you through the house will surely make him want to go.

As your dog matures, his workout can include some training, some games and some tricks. You can hide a biscuit and brush your teeth while your dog finds it. If he can't, when you finish your teeth, keep telling him "Find it," and walk close to where you hid it. Successful finds encourage longer searches. You can hide yourself. Especially if you have a walk-in closet.

You can combine any of the commands, tricks and games in this book with any of the ways you play with your dog to make up your own workout, changing it as your mood dictates. No matter what the content of your routine, the results will be the same—a more secure dog, a more tired dog, a dog with a better sense of humor, a more attentive dog, a dog who is content because he has been reminded of the order of his world. Just as we reassure our children that we will return soon and once again be attentive to their needs, the workout reassures your dog that everything is right in the world and should the need to worry arise, you will do it for him.

The small effort of the workout will make your dog feel *so* good. In fact, he may let you know when he's had enough, even before the 10 minutes is up, sighing contentedly and keeping the last toy you tossed to chew on before his nap.

Carol Lea Benjamin is the award-winning author and illustrator of seven previous Howell books on dog behavior and training, including *Mother Knows Best, The Natural Way To Train Your Dog* and *Surviving Your Dog's Adolescence*. She has taught dog behavior seminars all over the United States and in Canada, including a credit course for veterinarians at the 1994 New York State Veterinary Convention.

Ms. Benjamin is often a guest on radio and television and is frequently called on as an expert in dog behavior by authors and journalists. She is the winner of a Gaines "Fido," the first Kal Kan Pedigree Outstanding Pet Care Journalist Award, a New York State Humane Association ABC (A Book Can Develop Empathy) Award and The Dog Writers Association of America's highest honor, The Distinguished Service Award for Extraordinary Achievement and Communications Excellence.

Ms. Benjamin lives in New York City with her husband Stephen Lennard and their dogs Dexter and Flash.

Index

A